GLOBE FEARON

HIST_____UDIES

THE GREAT
MIGRATION
AFRICAN AMERICANS JOURNEY NORTH

GLOBE FEARON EDUCATIONAL PUBLISHER
Upper Saddle River, New Jersey
www.globefearon.com

CONSULTANTS

James Grossman is the Director of the Dr. William M. Scholl Center for Family and Community History at the Newberry Library in Chicago. He is the author of *Land of Hope: Chicago, Black Southerners, and the Great Migration* (honored with the Gustavus Myers Award for Outstanding Book on the Subject of Human Rights and the Illinois State Historical Society Award of Superior Achievement) and *A Chance to Make Good: African Americans 1900-1929*. He is the editor of the *Historical Studies of Urban America* series for the University of Chicago Press, and of *Black Workers in the Era of the Great Migration, 1916-1929*.

Nay Howell, certified in educational administration, curriculum, and supervision, has had careers in both the public and private sectors. In addition to being a training specialist with the city of Charlotte, North Carolina, she has a private consulting business for cultural diversity and developmental change. Nay has published *The Comprehensive Program Evaluation of Minority Achievements Program in the Charlotte-Mecklenburg Schools*.

Miriam J. Hines-Jiles teaches social studies at Lew Wallace High School in Gary, Indiana. She received her B.S. degree from Tuskegee University, a masters in African American Study-History at Clark-Atlanta University, and a masters in counseling and human development from Troy State University. Her particular field of interest is presenting the role of African American women in U.S. history. She has helped develop and implement the inclusion of African American studies across the curriculum in the Gary public schools.

David Katzman is chair of American Studies at the University of Kansas. His teaching and research focus on African American migration. He is the author of *Before the Ghetto: Black Detroit in the 19th Century* and *Seven Days a Week*. He is co-author of *A People and a Nation*.

Stephen A. Shultz is Assistant Principal Supervision/Social Studies at the Boys and Girls High School in Brooklyn, New York. Winner of the John Buzel Teacher of the Year Award in social studies for New York City high school teachers, he has had numerous fellowships from the Rockefeller Institute and Gilder Lehrman Institute for American history.

Executive Editor: Jean Liccione
Market Manager: Rhonda Anderson
Senior Editor: Karen Bernhaut
Project Editor: Lewis Parker
Writer: Barbara Somervill, Lewis Parker
Production Editor: Alan Dalgleish
Electronic Page Production: Mimi Raihl, Linda Bierniak, Phyllis Rosinsky
Photo Research: Jenifer Hixson, Martin A. Levick
Series and Cover Design: Joan Jacobus
Designer: Lisa Nuland

Printed in the United States of America 1 2 3 4 5 6 7 8 9 10 02 01 00 99 98

ISBN: 0-835-92311-8

GLOBE FEARON EDUCATIONAL PUBLISHER
Upper Saddle River, New Jersey
www.globefearon.com

CONTENTS

Between 1910 and the 1950s, millions of African Americans chose to journey North in the hope of changing their lives for the better.

THE GREAT MIGRATION

TERMS TO KNOW

- migration
- Great Migration
- Reconstruction
- Emancipation Proclamation
- Thirteenth Amendment
- cost of living

In 1914, 15-year-old Robert Fleming and his mother were cotton farmers in Alligator, Mississippi. When they were not working on their own farm, Robert helped grow cotton for other farms to earn extra money. Things were not easy for Robert. He said,

> I got in trouble with my boss. He took half my pay. I was making three dollars a week, working six in the morning to six at night.

Like many African American farm hands, Robert Fleming worked long hours for low pay. Somehow, he had managed to save $25, which he had hidden in a tree. He used this money to pay for his move out of Mississippi.

The first part of his **migration** was to Memphis, Tennessee, where he found work in an ice house. Migration is moving from one country or region to another. In the early 1900s, Memphis was a bustling industrial city, filled with music, a lively night life, and a large African American population. For Robert Fleming, Memphis was a three-year stop on the road to success.

Fleming was still a teenager when he joined the army and served in World War I. Once the war was over, he decided to settle in the North. By the age of 21, he had found his way to Cleveland, Ohio, and a job in a steel mill. The North seemed to offer Fleming everything that the South had denied him—a future filled with opportunity. He said,

I knew I would never do anything with my life living in Alligator. . . . So, when I left home, I had no intention of going back. I wanted to make it on my own.

Robert Fleming's story was a common one. From 1910 to 1929 and, again, from about 1940 to 1970, more than six and a half million African Americans migrated from the rural South. They had many reasons for migrating—freedom from discrimination, safety for their families, jobs and financial gain, education for their children, and the right to vote and to own property. Their hopes were centered on one goal—to achieve a better life in the North. The **Great Migration**, a shift in the African American population from rural South to urban North, was one of the largest movements of people in history.

No Equality for African Americans

After the Civil War, there were two phases of **Reconstruction**, or rebuilding the South. Under presidential Reconstruction, African Americans were excluded from exercising their civil rights, including voting. However, under Reconstruction plans set up by Congress between 1869 and 1877, African Americans achieved legal rights in the South equal to those of whites.

Many African Americans had hoped that President Abraham Lincoln's **Emancipation Proclamation**, which freed slaves in the South, would bring about immediate changes, but it did not do that. The **Thirteenth Amendment**, which abolished slavery, gave African Americans freedom guaranteed by law. However, laws did not change the attitudes and customs of whites in the South, and African Americans were disappointed

that freedom turned out to be less than they had expected.

During congressional Reconstruction, African American men actively voted and held government offices at all levels. In all, more than 600 African Americans were elected to Southern state legislatures during Reconstruction. African Americans were also elected to federal positions. For example, in 1870, Hiram Revels was sworn in as the first African American U. S. Senator.

Still, earning a living in the South for most African Americans was very difficult. Whites owned most of the land, and few African Americans could earn enough money to buy farm land. Those financially able to buy land discovered that most white landowners refused to sell to African Americans. With no land, their only avenue of employment was to work for a white plantation owner. In addition, because most Southern African Americans had only been trained to be farmers, their lack of education and money tied them to the South and agricultural work. Their gains in the South—legal rights, a more active role in government, and the promise of a better life—turned out to be temporary at best.

From Farm to City

By the 1880s, fearing African Americans' voting power, Southern whites used their control of state legislatures to put an end to freedom for African Americans. They passed state laws to control voting, education, and access to public places in an effort to weaken African American freedom.

Laws in the South also forced African Americans to live in a society that maintained "separate but equal" public facilities for whites and African Americans. The separate aspect was the most important factor for Southern whites—there was little interest in making public facilities equal. African Americans in the South were prohibited by law from using certain water fountains, rest rooms, buses, theaters, schools, or churches that were designated for white people. The desire for equality under the law became a focal point in the lives of Southern African Americans. On August 17, 1917, an editorial in the Dallas, Texas, *Express* stated,

The Negro is pleading to the South and the American people for justice and a square deal . . . . Let this country, the South in particular, reform its customs, habits of race prejudice. . .

As World War I began and many white workers joined the armed services, the North needed an inexpensive work force, and manufacturers looked to Southern African Americans to provide labor. The desire to leave the South together with the attraction of jobs in the North created a situation in which hundreds of thousands of African Americans decided migration was their best chance for success, even though migration meant leaving family, friends, and a familiar lifestyle. In Case Study 1, you will read more about those conditions in the South that caused African Americans to journey North.

Although the United States did not enter World War I until several years after the war had started in Europe, the war still had a major impact on Northern states. Factories in industrial centers of the North manufactured goods to be shipped to England and France. Manufacturers often paid transportation costs for workers to move North. Some business owners even provided migrants with one-way tickets to Chicago, Pittsburgh, or New York City. Case Study 2 describes ways that Southern African Americans learned about

opportunities that meant a chance for a new life in the North.

Families had to arrange their moves carefully. They saved their money, then sent one family member North to get settled before the entire family moved. African American migrants had little money and usually took the most direct route North. For example, African Americans living along the Atlantic coast usually traveled up the East Coast to cities like Philadelphia, New York City, and Boston. Many people from Georgia and Alabama traveled to Cleveland, Pittsburgh, and Detroit. Chicago received migrants from Mississippi and Louisiana. Railroads, such as the Illinois Central and the New York Central, carried migrants North. Others rode buses, cars, and trucks.

You will learn in Case Study 3 why many African Americans believed that migrating North would lead them to the "promised land," a place in which they would find freedom, opportunity, and a safe, happy life for their children.

For many migrants, the reality of the "promised land" didn't turn out as they thought. Few migrants realized that they would live in overcrowded city housing, work in jobs with little chance for promotion, and face yet another form of segregation and discrimination. Yet no matter what life was like in the North, few African Americans planned to return to the South. Consider

When the Great Migration started, many Southern African American sharecroppers lived in small cabins such as the one in this picture. Despite hardships in the South, the decision to start a new life in the North was not an easy one.

the opening lines of this poem (by Sparrell Scott, an African American migrant from the South), which was printed in the *Defender*, Chicago's African American newspaper:

When I Return to the Southland It Will Be
When lions eat grass like oxen
And an angleworm swallows a whale,
And a terrapin [tortoise] knits a woolen sock,
And a hare is outrun by a snail…

The Great Migration saw not only a shift from South to North but also a change in occupations for many African Americans. In the South, most African American males worked in farming. In the North, less than 6 percent of African American men worked in agriculture. The great majority were employed at unskilled or semiskilled jobs—stockyards, iron and steel mills, slaughter and packing houses, or as general laborers. The cycles of their lives changed—no longer did they work from spring to fall and then harvest a crop. Now their lives were dictated by the time clock and the assembly line. Case Study 4 focuses on the change in the kinds of jobs that African American migrants found.

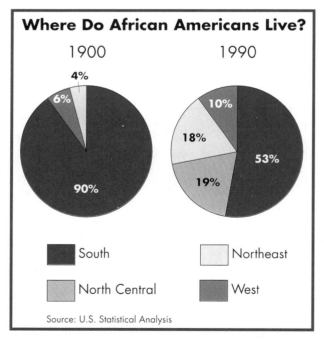

Where Do African Americans Live?

1900
4%
6%
90%

1990
10%
18%
53%
19%

■ South
■ North Central
□ Northeast
■ West

Source: U.S. Statistical Analysis

At the beginning of the 20th century, almost all African Americans lived in the South. The Great Migration changed that pattern. By 1990, which areas of the United States had gained in African American population?

The Struggle Against Injustice

To struggle against continuing prejudice and injustice, African Americans organized themselves into various groups. One of the primary organizations was the National Association for the Advancement of Colored People (NAACP). This organization fought battles in the courts to change racially biased laws.

The National Urban League worked to find housing and jobs for migrants. Marcus Garvey, a migrant from Jamaica, developed his Universal Negro Improvement Association (UNIA) to further African American pride and independence. You will read about these organizations and others in Case Study 5.

Harlem and Chicago

As the Great Migration picked up steam, the population of Northern cities grew at a fast rate. For example, New York City and Chicago drew African American migrants by the thousands. Harlem, in New York City, became the area with the largest African American population, taking in migrants from both the South and the Caribbean. In the 1920s, Harlem became the center for a blossoming of creativity and a rebirth of African American culture. Never before had so many talented African American artists, writers, and actors developed art that focused on African American experiences. Case Study 6 tells about the Harlem Renaissance and about the many creative people who contributed to it.

Chicago became the destination for many African Americans living in states along the Mississippi River. This increase in African Americans changed the culture of Chicago forever. As more and more African Americans came to live in Chicago, more and more businesses, restaurants, and clubs opened to serve the rising population. Political power rested in the hands of the newcomers, and before long they were electing their own representatives. Music, such as jazz and the blues, developed in Chicago. The Negro National Leagues and boxing champions such as Joe Louis showed that black athletes could rise above racial obstacles. You will read more about how the Great Migration changed Chicago in Case Study 7.

Transportation costs took much of the money that migrants saved for their trip North. Taking only what they could carry, these people rode North in the open back of a truck.

The Great Depression

As early as 1927, many African Americans began having trouble finding work. The Great Depression, which actually began in 1929, had hit African American migrants as early as two years before. The Great Depression, however, put an end to the vast numbers of African Americans migrating to the North. Because Northern cities had few jobs available and a higher **cost of living** than Southern farms, migrating North seemed pointless. The cost of living is the average price of food, housing, clothes, medical, and other essentials in a specific area. For migrants already in the North, the Depression brought on hard times. Rose Smith, an African American migrant living in Cleveland, said,

> *Depression times were real bad, real bad. . . . We sold hamburgers. . . . He [my husband] started out with a little steam-wagon and drove it all over town. He sold them so cheap, five and ten cents. . . . He was nice to the poor, the people who didn't have as much as we did. Sometimes he'd take scissors, tie clips and things from them if they didn't have any money. He hated to see anyone go hungry.*

A Good Book to Read

Up South, edited by Malaika Adero. New York: The New Press at CUNY, 1993.

Adero has collected a variety of primary source documents about the Great Migration. The book offers newspaper articles, essays, first-person experiences, and fiction to retell the story of 20th century African American migration.

The Second Wave: World War II and Beyond

Despite federal programs to end the Great Depression, financial hardship for all Americans lingered until the beginning of World War II in 1939. While the United States did not enter the war in 1939, U.S. factories geared up to provide manufactured goods to the Allies. Northern factories began hiring once again, and by the early 1940s, jobs opened up for African Americans in the North. Large numbers of Southern African Americans once again migrated to where they hoped better-paying jobs would mean a better lifestyle. They moved to Northern and Western manufacturing centers like New York City, Pittsburgh, Baltimore, Philadelphia, Cleveland, St. Louis, Los Angeles, Seattle, and Chicago.

African Americans joined the war effort, both in the military and on the home front. More than one million African Americans served in various branches of the military during the war. At the same time, factories that were desperate for workers hired African American men and women in huge numbers. African Americans again flocked to Northern cities and to the high pay offered by industry.

Then a new invention caused an even greater increase in migration. In 1944, a company named International Harvester introduced a mechanical cotton picker, one that replaced hand-pickers in the cotton fields. This machine made picking cotton faster and cheaper. By the 1950s, technology had changed Southern agriculture so dramatically that many African Americans were forced off farms. African Americans with no other job experience

The Great Depression hit African Americans especially hard—they had to struggle against both poverty and prejudice. In order to make a living, these migrants sold fruit at a stand in Washington, D.C.

found themselves out of work. Migration became the only answer. Consequently, the African American population wave again began to roll North. Case Study 8 explains how the second wave of migration affected Northern cities and the United States.

For migrants, conditions in Northern cities remained unchanged. In the workplace, African American migrants faced discrimination that prevented them from rising to better-paying positions. Many African Americans lived in overcrowded, broken-down housing. They openly resented being taken advantage of by landlords who ignored minimum standards for housing and health. Many migrants' children attended public schools with overcrowded classrooms, poor facilities, and unqualified teachers. The promise of the North for most migrants proved to be a lie.

Population Shifts

In 1910, 27 percent of the total African American population lived in urban centers across the country. By 1970, this number had jumped to 81 percent. Of the more than 22 million African Americans in the United States, almost 18 million lived in cities. In less than 100 years, the center of the African American population had shifted from the rural South to the urban North. As urban population expanded, public policies and facilities failed to keep pace. Housing, unemployment, education, and civil rights became focal issues for urban African Americans.

Along with their desire for a better life, African American migrants brought their history and culture with them as they moved North. African American music, art, and literature are important as part of modern America's cultural heritage.

Thinking It Over

1. What were some of the factors that caused African Americans to leave the South?
2. **Synthesizing** What historical events influenced the Great Migration?

Thousands of African Americans, tired of being taken advantage of by white landowners, decided to seek new beginnings in the North.

THE DREAM DENIED

CRITICAL QUESTIONS

- Why did many African Americans consider leaving the South in the early 1900s?
- How did African Americans in the South try to confront their social and economic problems?

TERMS TO KNOW

- sharecropping
- interest
- boll weevil
- segregated
- franchise
- lynching
- propaganda
- industrialized
- Exodusters

ACTIVE LEARNING

After reading this case study, you will write and present a skit about one cause for the African American migration out of the South. Look for political, social, and economic reasons for this migration.

After the Civil War, newly freed African Americans were hopeful about their future. During the war, enslaved African Americans were not allowed to own land. When the war ended, many thought of land ownership as the key to their freedom. They believed a rumor that the U.S. government would give them 40 acres of land and a mule. With land and the mule-power to work it, African American farmers would have a chance to provide for their families. But the dream of land ownership was not to come true for most African Americans.

The cost of land was high and the money earned by Southern African Americans was low, so most land remained in the hands of wealthy whites. Southern white landowners depended on cheap labor to work their fields. In order to keep African American farmers and poor whites attached to the land, they developed a system of farm labor called **sharecropping**.

Under the sharecropping system, most Southern African American farmers became tenants and worked land belonging to others. In payment for working the land, they were supposed to receive a share of the money made after the sale of the harvested crop. However, they were often cheated out of their share.

No one knew better than Nate Shaw the bitterness of the dream denied. Born in Alabama in 1885, from his teens, Shaw worked with fierce determination to succeed as a cotton farmer. But every time he got a bit ahead, something happened.

Eventually, Shaw joined an organization called the Sharecropper's Union. He hoped that by joining, he and other poor Southern farmers could begin to see economic justice done.

Acting on that belief, he stood his ground when a group of deputy sheriffs came to claim a fellow union member's property. Shaw defied them, shotgun in hand. For this act of defiance, he served 12 years in prison. When he got out, Shaw found his style of farming was outdated. Machines had replaced mules. The result was disastrous for him. He said,

> I never did have nothin' . . . . I ain't been able to save a penny. . . . I'm willin' to vow that I've never had a nickel in the bank in all the history of my life.

Shaw's experience with sharecropping was typical of that of many Southern African Americans.

In 1900, about 90 percent of all African Americans in the United States lived in the South. At that time, four-fifths of all Southern African Americans lived in rural areas and made their living working on the land. Between 1915 and 1930, more than a million African Americans left the South to live in Northern cities. There were many reasons why African Americans left the South to seek their dreams in the North. These dreams resulted in the Great Migration.

1 Sharecropping

During the late 1880s, in some states, such as Virginia and North Carolina, African American farmers planted tobacco. In other states, such as Louisiana, they grew sugarcane. Yet, throughout the South, cotton, as the major crop, was "king."

Owning land was very important to Southern African Americans. It was a right that had been denied to most of them. By 1900, about one-fourth of all Southern African Americans who worked on farms owned their land. Each year, the number of such African American farm owners increased due to their hard work and to their ability to save the money they made. Yet most farmers continued to rent their land and work as tenants in the sharecropping system.

A Good Book to Read

All God's Dangers: The Life of Nate Shaw by Theodore Rosengarten. New York: Alfred A. Knopf, 1975.

Nate Shaw's oral history gives vivid details of life as an African American sharecropper in the South.

This Southern sharecropper's family lived in a small cabin. The large pot served for both cooking food and washing clothes.

An Unfair System

Through the sharecropping system, a family farmed a part of the land belonging to another. They didn't own the crop; instead, they would get some of the profit when the crop was harvested and sold. Families had to sign contracts with landowners promising they would work on that particular farm until the crop was harvested. It was illegal to break the contract.

Sharecropper families most often lived in plantation cabins. These cabins, which contained no more than three rooms, were usually made of rough boards. If a cabin had windows, they were usually covered with paper. The cotton crop was grown right up to the door, so there was no space to plant a vegetable garden or raise animals.

In the spring, sharecroppers planted seed furnished by the planter with the landowners' tools. Because they could not raise their own food, they had to buy supplies and groceries. While the crop was growing, the family had little means of support because sharecroppers did not receive money as they worked. Most families had to buy supplies and food on credit at the local store, which was often owned by the landowner. They promised to pay their debt with the money made after the sale of the crop.

Sharecroppers also had to pay **interest** on their store debt. Interest is money a person has to pay for the use of borrowed money. Merchants often charged African Americans 40 to 70 percent interest, while white borrowers usually only paid about 4 percent. In addition, the landlord or merchant limited what a sharecropper could purchase.

Because sharecroppers signed contracts, they could not legally leave the farm where they worked until the harvest was complete. If they left, a sheriff could arrest them, put them in jail, and take their few possessions.

The harvest occurred in October and November. During those months, every family member usually worked from dawn to dusk, gathering cotton bolls, or seed pods, and dropping them into deep canvas bags.

The settlement of money and debts came in December. The landowner subtracted the family's debts from the share of the profits a sharecropper was supposed to receive. The settlement was almost always in favor of the white landowner—the sharecropper usually came out behind or made very little. Sometimes, the farmer wound up paying back money and even selling whatever the family owned to repay the debt. If a sharecropper protested that the settlement was unfair, a landowner might seize the sharecropper's property and drive him and his family off the plantation.

In reality, the sharecropping system was an unfair system that created a cycle of poverty and debt. Most African American families, like Moses

Burse's family, were trapped in a circle of debt from which there was no escape. Burse said,

> My dad would get in debt and he'd figure every year he going to get out. They'd tell you, "you bought so and so," they get through figuring it up you lacking $100 of coming clear. What could you do? You living on his place, you couldn't walk off.

Active Learning: Think about the problem of being a sharecropper. Take notes on sharecropping for use in your skit.

Plantation Hopping

There was no reason for a sharecropper to improve the family's living conditions on the farm where they worked. The little money that a sharecropper made was used to invest in making work easier, such as buying a wagon, a mule, or tools.

Although sharecroppers worked hard and had little interest in improving their lives on their landowners' farms, they were always looking for better opportunities that might exist at other farms. If conditions were absolutely terrible, sometimes they would travel to another plantation before the harvest. If caught, they faced jail or time on a chain gang. One Mississippi sharecropper recalled,

> I have knowed lots of people in Mississippi who cain't leave, because if you make a crop and don't clear nothin' and you still wound up owin' on your sharecrop and on your furnish' and you try to move, well the police be after you then all right.

After the harvest, they might try moving to another plantation. If a sharecropper had a debt, the debt followed from the former landowner to the new plantation, and it was added onto any debt that might result from the year's work there. However, some state laws forbade sharecroppers from leaving their plantations until their debts were paid.

Whether legal or not, there was constant movement of African Americans throughout the South. Some sharecroppers moved from farm to farm in the area where they lived. Others moved from county to county and state to state to where they thought landowners might offer better treatment.

Natural Disasters

While escaping debt grew more difficult for Southern farmers during and after World War I, natural disasters made it almost impossible to grow an abundant crop.

In 1915, terrible floods in Mississippi and Alabama destroyed crops, homes, and personal belongings. Farmers were forced off the land, and many left farm work forever.

Perhaps the worst natural disaster was the invasion of an insect called a **boll weevil**, a pest that lays eggs inside an unripe cotton boll. As young weevils eat their way out, they destroy the cotton.

Great swarms of boll weevils attacked cotton crops across South Carolina, Georgia, Alabama, Mississippi, Louisiana, and Texas. Boll weevils are insects that lay their eggs in cotton balls and destroy the crop. By 1922, the boll weevil had destroyed more than 85 percent of the cotton fields.

With their cotton fields in ruin, many landowners turned to planting corn. In order to harvest this crop, only about one-fifth as many workers were needed. Unemployment increased dramatically for African American farmers, causing thousands to give up farming and to head for possible jobs in Southern cities.

Thinking It Over

1. How did natural disasters control a farmer's life?
2. **Analyzing** What are some methods that landowners used to make sure that there was always a cheap labor source available to grow crops?

2 Jim Crow Laws

Immediately after the Civil War, there was a brief period of social and political progress for African Americans. The U. S. government passed two constitutional amendments to ensure their rights: the 14th Amendment, which granted all persons born or naturalized in the United States the rights of full citizenship, and the 15th Amendment, which stated that no citizen could be denied the right to vote because of race, color, or previous condition of servitude (slavery).

Segregation by Law

White lawmakers in the Southern states got around these amendments by passing laws called "Jim Crow" laws. These laws were named after a character in an African American minstrel show. "Jim Crow" became a Southern nickname for African Americans.

Under these laws, African Americans were **segregated**—forced to occupy separate sections of buses, trains, restaurants, and movie theaters. African Americans could not drink from the same public water fountains, could not be treated in the same hospitals, or buried in the same cemeteries as whites. If anyone challenged these laws, he or she risked prison or, in some cases, death.

The basic concept behind the "Jim Crow" laws was "separate, but equal facilities for all people." In 1896, in the case of *Plessy v. Ferguson*, the Supreme Court of the United States upheld the legality of "separate but equal" facilities, based on the Constitution. "Separate," however, rarely meant "equal" where African Americans were concerned.

Losing the Right to Vote

Immediately after the Civil War, African Americans received the right of **franchise**, or the right to vote, and many held elective office. But by the early 1900s, Southern lawmakers passed laws to restrict African Americans' right to vote. Some of these barriers included the following measures:

Poll tax. Some states required citizens to pay a poll tax in order to be able to vote. Poor farmers living on credit often found it impossible to pay such a tax.

Literacy test. Other states denied the vote to anyone unable to read or interpret a section of the state constitution. Many African Americans had never had the opportunity to learn to read, so they were denied the vote, while white election

Jim Crow laws separated whites and African Americans in Southern society. State laws kept African Americans from using the same parks, taxis, and telephone booths as whites. According to Jim Crow laws, African Americans could not even drink from the same public water fountains as whites.

registrars might tell those who could read that their interpretation of the constitutional passage was "unsatisfactory."

Grandfather clause. This clause allowed anyone whose grandfather had been a voter to also vote. Since African Americans had no voting "grandfathers," they did not qualify under this clause. The grandfather clause, by allowing for more white voters, meant whites would continue to control state governments and determine whom to send as representatives to the federal government.

Property test. This requirement meant that a man must own a certain amount of property in order to vote. Few African Americans and poor whites could meet this requirement.

White primary elections. Primary elections are elections that nominate candidates for an office. White primary elections allowed Southern Democrats to ban African American men because primary elections were not covered by the 15th Amendment.

These ways to eliminate the franchise for African Americans worked. Among Alabama's 181,471 African Americans eligible to vote in 1900, only 3,000 were registered. Other Southern states had similar ratios of registered-to-eligible voters.

The freedom to vote became yet another reason for migrating North. For those who were never allowed to vote in the South, casting their votes in a Northern election became a symbol of their new lives.

A Good Video to Watch

"Any Place But Here" Episode One of *The Promised Land*. Discovery Communications, 1996.

This video, based on the book The Promised Land by Nicholas Lemann, highlights economic, political, and social injustices suffered by African Americans in the "cotton belt" of Mississippi.

Active Learning: Traveling under Jim Crow laws was difficult for African Americans. Consider a situation with an African American migrant traveling by train. What problems would this person face? Take notes on Jim Crow laws to use in your skit.

3 Seeking a Better Education

Freed African Americans were eager to educate themselves and their children. During the late 1800s, almost 4,500 schools for African Americans were built throughout the South. In spite of relatively high fees, enrollment soared to 250,000 within just a few years.

In the early 1870s, these schools were replaced by public schools that were attended by both African Americans and whites. However, with "Jim Crow" laws in effect, schools in the South, like other public facilities, became strictly segregated.

Although African Americans paid their share of taxes, most tax money went to build and maintain white schools. Most African American schools were crowded, run-down, and had few supplies for students. For instance, in Alabama's African American schools, there was one teacher for every 65 students. In rural communities, classes were often held in sharecroppers' cabins, stores, or churches. African American teachers were often poorly educated; only a few of them had more than an eighth grade education

In addition, teachers were always underpaid, as shown by this letter from a Lexington, Mississippi, teacher, written May 12, 1917:

I was educated at Alcorn College and have been teaching a few years; but, ah, me, the Superintendent under whom we poor colored teachers have to teach cares less for a colored man than he does for the vilest beast. I am compelled to teach 150 children without any assistance and receives only $27 a month, the white [teachers work] with 30 [students] and get $100.

A Separate, Unequal Opportunity

School terms for African Americans and poor whites were short. At planting and harvest time, plantation owners pressured farmers to keep their children from school and put them to work in the fields. Nate Shaw blamed this practice for his own lack of education. The planters' attitude was, he said,

> "Send the children to school till we say quit—and when we say quit . . . quit!" Into the white man's field we'd have to go. None of my brothers and sisters, not one of them by name, got a good book learnin.'

Few students went on to high school because African American secondary schools were rare. In 1915, Mississippi, Alabama, Georgia, and Louisiana had a total of six public high schools for African Americans. In North Carolina, greater attention was paid to educating African Americans than in most Southern states. Yet in the late 1920s, even there, more money was spent on buying buses for white schools than on building new schools for African American students.

One positive movement for African American education was the Julius Rosenwald Fund. Between 1913 and 1932, more than 5,000 African American schools were built, and 15 percent of the money came from this private fund. However, most African Americans were educated in an inferior school system that kept them in low-paying jobs.

Many African Americans were anxious to migrate and do any kind of work so that they could live in a place where they could educate their children.

Active Learning: The education offered to African Americans in the South contrasted greatly with the education available to whites. Take notes on African American education in the South for use in your skit.

4 Fear and Violence

The hardest lesson for Southern African Americans to learn was to live with fear for their personal safety. On a day-to-day basis, many law-abiding African Americans were fearful of just walking public streets by themselves, as they might be insulted, attacked, and beaten for no reason.

As education improved for most whites in the South, education for African Americans did not keep pace. For example, schools for African Americans did not have adequate facilities. In many schools, 50 or more students of all ages had classes in one large room with one teacher.

The fear of attack and random violence by Southern whites provided another reason why many African Americans migrated North. As the Houston *Observer* noted:

Take some of the sections from which the Negro is departing and he can hardly be blamed when the facts are known. He is kicked around, cuffed, lynched, burned, homes destroyed, daughters insulted and oftimes raped, has no vote nor voice, is underpaid, and in some instances when he asks for pay receives a 2 x 4 over his head. . . . When such conditions are placed and forced upon a people and no protest is offered, you cannot blame a race of people for migrating.

Whitecapping

In some instances, where African Americans did own their own land, groups of whites pushed the African Americans off their land by threatening violence. These whites usually struck the homes of successful African Americans during the night. Because the attackers often wore white caps as part of their disguise, the practice was called "whitecapping."

Sometimes these whitecappers would force whole communities of African Americans from their homes. Between 1880 and 1900, at least 239 instances of whitecapping were recorded, with the largest number occurring in Mississippi.

Lynching

For defying the system, acting uppity, or even for no reason at all, an African American could be the target of an angry mob. Punishment might range from tarring and feathering to being forced from one's home or having one's home or crops burned—or even **lynching**. A lynching is when a mob illegally seizes and kills, usually by hanging, a suspected criminal or troublemaker.

Between 1889 and 1918, approximately 3,209 people were lynched in the United States; 219 in the North, 156 in the West, and 2,834 in the South. Of those lynched, 2,522 were African Americans. People were lynched for everything from breaking

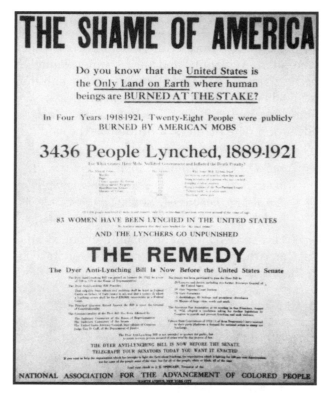

Many African American organizations urged Congress to pass federal laws against lynching.

a sharecropping contract to shooting rabbits. However, lynching was not done just to create terror. White Southerners carried out lynchings in order to preserve their position of authority in the community.

Among those speaking out against lynchings was Ida B. Wells-Barnett. Born enslaved in Mississippi, she became the editor and part owner of a Memphis, Tennessee, newspaper called *Free Speech*. In her newspaper, she wrote articles condemning lynchings. In 1895, she published the *Red Record*, which contained statistics and detailed descriptions of lynchings. One horrifying description she gave was the lynching of Henry Smith, an accused murderer. She wrote,

Arriving here at 12 o'clock the train was met by a surging mass of humanity 10,000 strong. The Negro was placed upon a carnival float in mockery of a king upon his throne, and, followed by an immense crowd, was escorted through the city so that all might see the most

inhuman monster known in current history. . . . Smith was placed upon a scaffold. . . . securely bound, within the view of all beholders. Here the victim was tortured for fifty minutes. . . . Then, being apparently dead, kerosene was poured upon him, cottonseed hulls placed beneath him and set on fire.

Although lynching became a topic of national concern, no effective anti-lynching legislation was passed. After the lynching of three African American store owners in Memphis, Ida Wells-Barnett wrote,

There is only one thing left we can do—leave a town which will neither protect our lives and property nor give us a fair trial, but take us out and murders us in cold blood.

Some whites, angry at Wells-Barnett's comments, threatened to lynch her. However, she was in New York at the time. Instead, a mob, which included many important Memphis citizens, destroyed her printing presses.

Mob violence was not directed only at poor, uneducated African Americans, nor did all violence end in lynching. In 1906, after a race riot in Atlanta, whites attacked Jesse Max Barber, editor of the *Voice of the Negro.* Barber was given three choices: leave town, take back his comments about the causes of the riot, or serve on a chain gang. Like Ida Wells-Barnett, Barber chose to leave.

The Rise of the Ku Klux Klan

Closely connected to the lynchings and random violence in the South was the rise of a white secret society called the Ku Klux Klan. The KKK used Southern whites' fears to provoke mob violence against African Americans. KKK **propaganda,** which is false or distorted information, tried to convince Southern whites that African Americans were naturally violent people. In this way, the KKK excused its own often violent attacks on African Americans.

Men disguised in white robes and hoods made night raids on the homes and families of African Americans, urged mobs to form for lynchings, and burned crosses in the yards of those who opposed their tyranny. Besides violence, the KKK held a strong political position in the South,

fighting for white power and against progress for African Americans.

White prejudice and the threat of violence caused many African Americans to fear for their lives. The fear of lynching was very real. Seeking safety for themselves and their children, many African Americans headed North.

5 Moving Out

Even before the Great Migration started, many African Americans had moved off the plantations to Southern towns and cities to work in business and industry. African Americans set up small businesses, including food stores, restaurants, drugstores, cigar

Ku Klux Klan members disguised themselves before their raids. They used violence, arson, and murder in their reign of terror against African Americans.

stores, dry-cleaners, and shoe-repair shops. African American beauty salons, barbershops, and mortuaries provided services to the community. In addition, banks and insurance companies owned by African Americans prospered. For example, the North Carolina Mutual Life Insurance company in Durham, North Carolina, became the largest U.S. business owned and operated by African Americans. These businesses formed the beginning of a growing African American middle class.

Unfortunately, African American-owned businesses did not have an easy road to success, and many failed. The main reasons for failure were the lack of funding, the lack of business experience, the tendency to offer too much credit, and poor location.

Active Learning: Imagine that you and your family are being forced off your land. Consider what you would do and say in this situation.

Thinking It Over

1. How did Southern states get around the terms of the 15th Amendment?
2. **Drawing Conclusions** Why do you think so few Southern-born African Americans received a good education?

The Lure of the Cities

Between 1880 and 1915, the first wave of African American migration from the South occurred. Some African Americans were pulled to cities and towns in the North and West by the promise of better-paying jobs. During the last half of the 19th century, the United States became more **industrialized**. The country was developing an economy based on industries and manufacturing.

At first, most industry was located in cities of the Northeast and Midwest. In many of these communities, African Americans competed for jobs with recent immigrants from Europe. Usually the Europeans got the jobs. Gradually, Northerners invested money in the South, attracted by the region's cheap labor and rich natural resources. At this time, many African Americans left their farms for better jobs in cities like Birmingham and Atlanta.

Roads West

For thousands of African Americans, the West seemed to hold great promise as a place to start life over. The largest mass movement West was led by Henry Adams of Louisiana and Benjamin "Pap" Singleton of Tennessee. They believed the economic future for African Americans lay in setting up separate, self-supporting communities. In addition, the West offered free land. Under the Homestead Act of 1862, settlers could receive grants of 160 acres of public land on the Great Plains if they lived on and farmed the land for five years.

All Colored People
THAT WANT TO
GO TO KANSAS,
On September 5th, 1877,
Can do so for $5.00

Handbills helped to attract African American settlers to lands in the West. This handbill was passed out in Lexington, Kentucky, in 1877.

Pap Singleton's group started their first colony at Nicodemus, Kansas. In the 1880s, Nicodemus had several schools and a church. It also had dozens of businesses, including Williams General Merchandise shown in this photo.

In 1879 and 1880, Adams, Singleton and others led African Americans to the prairie lands of Kansas. These migrants called themselves **Exodusters** after the title of the Book of Exodus in the Bible, which described the Israelites' exodus, or flight, from Egypt to the Promised Land.

In time, as many as 50,000 Exodusters went to Kansas and other western areas, such as Colorado and California. Between 1890 and 1916, more than 30 towns with large African American populations sprang up in Oklahoma. Many of these towns prospered. For example, soon after African Americans established Boley, Oklahoma, in 1904, the town had two banks, a sawmill, a cotton gin, three newspapers, two hotels, and a college. In addition, hundreds of African American settlers also moved to the Great Plains region farther west and north.

Heading North

Although life continued to be difficult for the many African Americans who migrated, they found freedoms that had been denied to them in the South. Letters to family and friends encouraged others to consider the opportunities that waited for them outside the South.

In all, over 330,000 African Americans left the South between 1870 and 1900, but that was just the beginning. Between 1914 and 1918, hundreds of thousands of African Americans decided to journey North, where there were opportunities for work, education, and a new life.

A Good Movie to See

The Autobiography of Miss Jane Pittman. Starring Cicely Tyson, this movie is available in VHS.

This video covers the fictitious life of an 110-year-old African American woman in the South. The story covers her life from the Civil War through the start of the Civil Rights Movement.

Thinking It Over

1. Why did many African Americans move West?
2. **Analyzing** What role did industrialization play in the movement of African Americans to the cities?

GOING TO THE SOURCE

One More Bale: A Tale About the Sharecropping System

African Americans managed to take the edge off their bitterness with a sense of humor. Below is a story repeated so often in the South that it became a sort of folk tale. It involves a planter, whom the sharecroppers called "Mr. Charlie," and an African American farmer named Joe. In some years, Joe raised ten or twelve bales of cotton. In other years, his crop produced only seven or eight bales. But no matter how much cotton he raised, he always ended up in debt. One year he dreamed up a way to test the system. This is the story of how Joe put Mr. Charlie to the test.

When the harvest came, Joe produced seven bales. Mr. Charlie appeared and went through his usual ritual with pencil and paper. "Well," he said, "it's not too bad. What with the expenses and the money I advanced you, plus last year's debt, and the interest and all, it works out close. Mighty close. One more bale, and you'd be dead even."

Joe favored his employer with a disarming smile. "Boss, I've been with you many a year, and you know I wouldn't cheat you. No, sir. But I was funning you a little. I've got another bale. It's stashed out yonder, in the weeds."

Mr. Charlie was only mildly annoyed. "Doggone it," he said. "You've put me to a lot of trouble. Now I have to figure the whole thing over again." When he had adjusted his calculations, he said, "Well, now, there are some items I near forgot, like charging you a little something for the use of the plow. But no matter. It all balances out. You still owe me one more bale."

1. What does this story tell about the sharecropping system?
2. What does Joe know about the planter?
3. What would happen if Joe found another bale in the barn?
4. Why doesn't Joe just sell his extra bale someplace else?
5. **Analyzing a Story** How would this story encourage someone to migrate to the North or West?

Case Study Review

Identifying Main Ideas

1. List all the reasons that motivated African Americans to leave the South.
2. What conditions made it difficult for African American farmers to earn a living in the South after the Civil War?
3. How did Southern whites use violence to control African Americans?

Working Together

Form a small group with three or four classmates. Review this case study and create a poster about one aspect of the treatment of African Americans in the South from 1880 to 1915. This poster should present the African American point of view. On the back of the poster, write two or three reasons why you think African Americans felt the way they did. Present your poster to the class.

Active Learning

Writing a Skit Working in a small group, write and present a skit about one cause for the African American migration from the South. Make sure each person in your group has a role in the skit. You can choose to enact an economic, social, or political cause. Be sure to explain your cause as you write the dialogue for your skit. Practice your skit, then present it to the class.

Lessons for Today

Southern-born African Americans were frequent victims of lynchings, burnings, beatings, and other hate crimes. African Americans and other groups today continue to experience first-hand acts of racial hatred. What steps should police officers and other public officials take to stop hate crimes and to ensure the personal safety of all citizens?

What Might You Have Done?

The year is 1907. Imagine you are a well-educated African American returning home to the rural South. You are very thirsty, but there is only one public water fountain around, and it is marked "For Whites Only." Would you take a drink? Why? What would you expect to happen if you did drink?

Questioning Unfair Attitudes, Opinions, and Beliefs

The Language of Thinking

A critical reader looks beyond the words a writer or speaker presents to the meaning behind the words. A person's attitudes and beliefs are the result of many things: parents, family, friends, religion, school, community, reading habits, and so on.

As you read, try to uncover the reasons why people think the way they do.

You have probably met people who have attitudes, opinions, or beliefs that are harmful to others. It takes great courage to speak out against unjust opinions. To do so, you have to listen to and honestly consider other points of view. By honestly considering why people feel or believe as they do, you remain fair and open-minded. This can help you recognize the truth and form opinions of your own.

The following passage is taken from *Colored People: A Memoir*, by Henry Louis Gates, Jr. In this passage, Mr. Gates talks about growing up in the segregated town of Piedmont, West Virginia:

> *For most of my childhood, we couldn't eat in restaurants or sleep in hotels, we couldn't use certain bathrooms or try on clothes in stores. Mama insisted that we dress up when we went to shop. She was a fashion plate when she went to clothing stores, and wore white pads called shields under her arms so her dress or blouse would show no sweat. We'd like to try this on, she'd say carefully. . . We don't buy clothes we can't try on, she'd say when they declined, as we'd walk, in Mama's dignified manner, out of the shop.*

> *I hated the fact that we couldn't sit down in the Cut-Rate. . . . You were supposed to stand at the counter, get your food to go, and leave. . . . Even after basketball games . . . the colored players had to stand around and drink out of paper cups while the white players and cheerleaders sat down in the red Naugahyde booths and drank out of glasses. Integrate? I'll shut it down first, owner Carl Dadisman had vowed. . . . He didn't want us sitting in his booths, eating off his plates and silverware, putting our thick greasy lips over all his glasses. He'd retire first, or die.*

Think about the ways in which people voice their opinions. Then answer the questions below:

1. **Analyzing** How did Henry feel about segregation in his hometown? How do you know?

2. **Understanding Points of View** According to what the whites of Piedmont thought, was Henry's family treated fairly? Why do you think so?

3. **Forming an Opinion** Would you speak out against segregation if you were Henry? Why?

4. How have you changed your opinions or beliefs in the last year or two?

After packing their possessions, these African Americans were ready to start on their journey North.

YEARS OF CRISIS, TIME OF HOPE

CRITICAL QUESTIONS

- How did World War I help trigger the Great Migration?
- In what ways did African Americans learn about life in the North?

TERMS TO KNOW

- sharecropper
- recruiters
- immigrants
- circulation
- industrialists
- exodus

ACTIVE LEARNING

After you read this case study, you will write an editorial for an African American newspaper being published during World War I. In your editorial, you will give reasons why you think African Americans living in the South should migrate to Northern cities. For an editorial, you need to write a statement of opinion and to support it with some facts. As you read this case study, take notes that will help you support your position.

It was a warm April day in 1917. People on the streets of large cities stopped and listened when they heard newspaper sellers yelling, "Paper! Get your paper! War declared! Read all about it! The U.S. is at war!"

Ida May Johnson probably did not hear about the war as she cleaned her small cabin home near Macon, Georgia. Television had not yet been invented. Radios were not common. Even a newspaper would have done Ida May little good; she could not read.

Even if she had heard the news, Ida May might not have given it much thought. Ida May's worries focused only on surviving. She was a widow with two teenage sons and enough troubles of her own. Her husband had been a **sharecropper**. A sharecropper rents another person's land and is given credit to buy supplies and food. In return for growing crops, the sharecropper gets a share of the profits when the crops are sold and uses the money to pay bills.

The Johnson family was trying to work the farm, but they were struggling. Swarms of insects called boll weevils had begun attacking the cotton. Without a crop, how would she pay for the food she had bought on credit?

A year after the war started in Europe, in 1915, Ida May's older son had left home to work in the steel mills of Pittsburgh. In 1917, her other son joined the U.S. Army. A year later, Ida May herself migrated to Pittsburgh to live with her son.

In just a few years, a war that had started a world away changed Ida May Johnson's life forever. It changed as well the lives of thousands of other African Americans living in cities and towns in the South and in the North.

1 World War I Spurs the Great Migration

World War I (1914–1918) caused a huge movement of African Americans from the towns and fields of the South to the cities and factories of the North. So many African Americans took part in this movement that it has become known as the Great Migration. Ida May Johnson and her older son were only two of more than a million African Americans who took advantage of new opportunities in the North.

The United States at War

At first, World War I involved only countries in Europe, not the United States. The Central Powers—Germany, the Austro-Hungarian Empire, and Italy—fought against the Allies—France, Russia, and Great Britain. Because the war eventually involved countries in all parts of the world, it became known as a world war.

After Germany attacked U.S. ships in 1917, the United States entered the war on the side of the Allies. By the end of the war, about 380,000 African Americans had served in the U.S. armed services.

In the U.S. Army, African Americans served in regiments usually commanded by white officers. However, most African Americans were not allowed to fight. Instead, they were assigned the worst physical jobs, such as building warehouses, driving trucks, and digging graves. Ida May's son, in the 93rd Regiment, was one of the few African American soldiers allowed to fight. They fought bravely, and by the end of the war, about 40,000 African Americans had seen combat duty.

Workers Wanted on the Home Front

Before the United States entered the war, the Allies had asked the United States for help. To meet these demands, U.S. factories began to increase production of wartime goods—uniforms, canned foods, and the steel that was used in making ships, tanks, weapons, and ammunition.

At the same time that demands on American companies increased, a sudden labor shortage took place. The war caused a sharp decrease in the numbers of **immigrants** coming to the United States. Immigrants are people who move to another country to live. Before the war, many factory jobs had been filled by recent immigrants from Europe. After the war broke out, fewer people could safely move to the United States because enemy ships prowling the seas made travel too dangerous.

The 369th Infantry was one of the African American regiments allowed to fight—but only alongside French troops, not with U.S. forces. After World War I, the 369th returned to New York City. For their bravery in battle, each soldier received the French medal of honor.

The war also caused a drain on white Northern workers. They were no longer available to fill job openings in factories. Millions of men were serving in the armed forces and fighting in Europe.

U.S. companies, mostly located in the North, faced a serious problem. Where were they going to find enough workers to meet wartime demands?

Thinking It Over

1. What jobs did African American soldiers do in World War I?
2. **Drawing Conclusions** How could a war in Europe affect the migration of people in the United States?

Active Learning: What new opportunities did the war create for African Americans? Write down a few phrases to use in your editorial.

2 Recruiting Southern Workers

Northern factory owners soon found a solution to the labor shortage. They decided to encourage whites and African Americans in the South to take the jobs. To attract Southern workers, Northern **industrialists**, or manufacturers, hired labor **recruiters**. A recruiter is an agent whose job it is to find new members to join or enroll in a specific group. These recruiters were mostly African Americans who traveled throughout the South hoping to persuade people to work in the North. In the early years of the war, the recruiters mainly represented industries that immediately needed workers, such as steel mills, meat packing houses, and railroads.

A Glowing Picture

The recruiters promised jobs that paid $5 a day. Southern farm workers usually made less than $1 a day, and factory workers in the South made about 14 cents an hour. By going North, workers could earn in a day what they had made in a week in the South. Before the war, for example, Ida May

Johnson's family lived on about $290 a year—the average yearly income in rural Georgia at that time. In Pittsburgh in 1918, both she and her son would have been able to earn between $3.00 and $3.60 a day or at least $720 a year. The Johnson family wanted a better life. Moving north to Pittsburgh seemed to be the answer to their dreams.

Besides the high wages, recruiters painted a glowing, and often unrealistic, picture of life in the North. One recruiter in Birmingham, Alabama published the following advertisement:

> *Let's go north where there are no labor troubles. Good wages, fair treatment. Two weeks pay. Good houses. We ship you and your household goods. Will advance you money if necessary. Scores of men have written us thanking us for sending them. Go now while you have the chance.*

Trying to Stop the Flow

Alarm spread throughout the South as white employers saw tens of thousands of African American farm laborers and household workers pack up and head North. Most Southern communities did not react well to this migration.

World War I caused a job shortage in the North. The shipyards on Hog Island near Philadelphia advertised steady work and good wages.

A Good Book to Read

Bound for the Promised Land by Michael L. Cooper. New York: Lodestar Books, 1995.

The author uses many first-person accounts to tell the story of the Great Migration. Photos bring to life this exodus, which changed forever the face of America.

Instead of encouraging African Americans to stay in the South, they turned to threats and violence to stop the migration.

Some towns passed laws requiring recruiters to buy licenses. A license might cost thousands of dollars. For example, towns in South Carolina, Florida, and Alabama charged between $1,000 and $2,000 for a license. In Macon, Georgia, a license cost $25,000. After paying for a license, the applicant still had to be approved by 10 local ministers, 10 manufacturers, and 25 local business people!

Recruiting without a license was usually subject to stiff fines and sometimes jail sentences. For instance, in Montgomery, Alabama, the penalty was a $100 fine and six months at hard labor in the prison. In Jacksonville, Florida, the punishment was a $600 fine and 60 days in jail. In some places, agents were arrested and beaten.

In spite of such efforts, recruiters continued to come, and African Americans continued to leave the South. It was a tide of people on their journey North. As one reporter remarked at the time, "They might as well have tried to stop [by law] the migration of the boll weevil."

African Americans Against Migration

Not all African Americans living in the South thought that migration was a good idea. Many African American educators, ministers, and business people urged people to stay where they were. Just two years before the outbreak of the war, Booker T. Washington, an influential African American leader and the president of Tuskegee Institute, had written:

> [I have] never seen any part of the world where it seemed to me the masses of the Negro people would be better off than right here in these southern states.

Robert R. Moton, who replaced Washington at Tuskegee Institute, held similar views. He believed that the majority of African Americans were better suited to farming than to any other way of life. He made speeches declaring that it was the patriotic duty of African American sharecroppers to stay at home and produce food for the troops fighting in Europe.

Other African American leaders felt that migrants would find life more difficult in the North than in the South. For example, Kelly Miller, a professor at Howard University, predicted that

when the war ended, Northern employers would fire African American migrants and rehire white soldiers returning from the war. An article in the *Tuskegee Negro Farmer* warned that in the North, African Americans would "find themselves finally entangled in the great web of disappointment, misery, and crime."

Active Learning: What were reasons why African Americans might have wanted to leave the South? How could you have argued against African American leaders who tried to persuade people to remain in the South? Write down these arguments to use in your editorial.

Thinking It Over

1. What arguments did labor recruiters use to convince Southern African Americans to move to the North?
2. **Understanding Points of View** Who opposed migration to the North, and why?

Booker T. Washington was the best-known African American educator and leader of his time. He believed that Southern African Americans should remain in the South and develop friendly relationships with whites.

3 Spreading the Word

Although some people spoke against migration, many more promoted moving to the North. Encouragement for the Great Migration came from letters from family members and friends who had gone North to find work, visits home from family members who had already made the move, church ministers, and newspaper accounts.

Letters and Visits Home

Sometimes the inspiration to leave home came from a letter describing the freedom and opportunity a friend had found in the North. One man wrote the following letter:

I should have been here twenty years ago. I just begin to feel like a man . . . My children are going to the same school with the whites and I don't have to humble to no one. I have registered. Will vote in the next election and there isn't any yes Sir and no Sir. It's all yes and no, Sam and Bill.

Sometimes the will to move was born when a family member returned to the South for a special event, such as a wedding or funeral. At these times, everyone would celebrate. Homecoming migrants dressed in their very best city-bought clothes. They tried to impress the "home folks" with exciting— and sometimes exaggerated—tales of life in the North. One man who had moved from St. Helena Island, South Carolina, to Harlem in New York City, recalled such an occasion:

Everybody knows when I go home. My mother's house can't hold all the people. I have set up all night talking to the people down there about the things I've seen up here. Then when I finish one or two of them will say, "Uncle Joe, can't you take me back up there with you?"

The Community Church

In the South, the church had always been the center of most social activities in rural towns. Southern farmers traveled miles to come to church to worship, see friends, and catch up on the news. Church ministers who had attended regional and national conventions brought back regional and national news to share with their congregations. They told them about members who had moved away and about job opportunities in Northern cities. Some ministers used the information they learned to encourage members to make the journey North, giving them letters of introduction to churches in the North.

The Power of the Press

In the days before radio or television, newspapers provided an important source of information for all Americans. By 1920, more than 280 newspapers and magazines published mainly for African Americans existed—at least one in every city with a large African American population. Even people who could not read were not cut off from the news. Someone would read the newspaper to those who could not read. Ida May Johnson and her sons, for example, could have listened as someone read a newspaper aloud in a church, barbershop, or pool hall. After listening to the newspaper accounts, listeners discussed the articles.

Most African American newspapers published in the South were not good sources of information about the Great Migration. Their editors had too much to lose if local white Southerners disapproved of their opinions on the subject. Whites who disagreed with the newspaper articles might burn down the newspaper office or harm the editors or their families.

During visits home for family reunions, people talked about life in the North. Relatives and neighbors who had moved North helped to persuade others to migrate.

Instead, the most powerful source of information was a Northern newspaper called the *Chicago Defender*. Robert Abbott, an African American who started the *Defender*, was its editor and publisher. He was driven by two passions: freedom for his people and fame for his newspaper.

The *Defender* had a dramatic writing style and the largest **circulation** of any African American newspaper in the nation. Circulation is the number of newspapers or magazines sold within a given period. Between 1916 and 1919, its paid circulation went from 33,000 to 130,000 subscribers. It is estimated that each week it made its way to some 1,500 Southern cities and towns where it was passed house to house to the point of being worn out.

Delivering the News

Many white Southerners feared and hated the *Defender*'s influence and tried to block its distribution. White groups prevented mail carriers from delivering the newspaper. People caught selling it were often beaten or jailed. In Georgia, a young boy selling the *Defender* was murdered.

Robert Abbott fought back. He enlisted the help of railroad workers and entertainers. Each week, railroad workers, such as Pullman porters and dining-car waiters, brought hundreds of copies of the newspaper from Chicago. Traveling actors and musicians also stuffed copies of the *Defender* into their luggage. Then these people delivered the newspapers to local distributors at train stops.

When introducing the *Defender* to a community for the first time, distributors often handed out free copies. After church services, many ministers gave away issues of the newspaper. Barbers put out copies for their customers. Actors sometimes persuaded ushers to pass out copies to members of their audiences. In these ways, news of the Great Migration continued to spread throughout the South.

The Great Exodus

The journalists at the *Defender* painted a picture of the Great Migration that appealed to people's emotions. They compared the movement to the **exodus** of the Israelites from Egypt, as described in the Bible. Exodus is the Biblical word for departure.

The *Defender*, which called itself the "World's Greatest Weekly," had great popular appeal. The front page had sensational headlines printed in red ink. A column called "Below the Mason Dixon Line" featured horror stories of injustice against African Americans throughout the South. The *Defender* included songs and poems with such titles as "Land of Hope" and "Bound for the Promised Land," which reinforced the idea of a better life in the North.

The *Defender*'s readers also enjoyed descriptions of the marvels of life in the North. They read about Chicago's Wendell Phillips High School, which offered its pupils science labs, literary clubs, and debating societies. Such schools were a far cry from public schools in the South, many of them housed in sharecroppers' cabins. Articles told about Provident Hospital, where patients could receive the most up-to-date medical care from African American doctors, nurses, and administrators. Sports pages featured stories about the games of Chicago's African American baseball team and the boxing matches of Chicago's own Jack Johnson.

The *Defender* was as popular then as the most popular TV program today. As a New Orleans woman declared, *[I] had rather read it than to eat when Saturday comes, it is my heart's delight.*

"We Want Out!"

As the *Defender*'s circulation rose, hundreds of letters poured into its office from African American readers. Some people asked for information. Many asked for help in finding jobs. In almost all the letters, people expressed despair over their old life in the South and hope for a better life in the North.

For example, a teenager from Anniston, Alabama expressed his hopes for the future:

Dear Sir: I saw your add in the Chicago Defender for laborers. I am a young man and want to finish school. I want you to look out for me a job on the place working morning and evening. I would like to get a job in some private family so I could continue taking my piano lesson I can do anything around the house but drive and can even learn that.

A young artist from Palestine, Texas, wrote:

Sirs: this is somewhat a letter of information I am a colored Boy aged 15 years old and I am talented for an artist and I am in search of some one will Cultivate my talent I have studied Cartooning therefore I am a Cartoonist and I intend to visit Chicago this summer and I want to keep in touch with your association and too from you knowledge can a Colored boy be an artist and make a white man's salary up there.

These letters and many more show the important role played by the *Chicago Defender* in encouraging the Great Migration. But the *Defender* was only one source of information about opportunities in the North. The word was spread through the mighty voices of labor recruiters, friends, family members, and ministers. Within just a few years, these voices helped to persuade over a million African Americans to leave the South and seek new lives in the cities of the North.

Active Learning: Take notes on the cultural and educational opportunities available in Northern cities. You may want to cite these opportunities as reasons for Southern families to move North.

Thinking It Over

1. In what ways did friends and relatives of African Americans create interest in the Great Migration?
2. **Drawing Conclusions** Why did some white Southerners try to block distribution of the *Defender?*

During World War I, Southern African Americans headed North looking for jobs. Riveting steel beams in a shipyard was a well-paying job in the North.

GOING TO THE SOURCE

Northward Bound

Photographs can help you understand a period of time in ways that words sometimes cannot. Pictures provide clues to the past and a feel for the time. They show us how people and places in recent history looked.

The *Chicago Defender's* campaign for Northern migration began in earnest in 1916. The picture and caption below appeared on the front page of the paper on September 2, 1916. Study the picture and the caption. Then answer the questions that follow.

The original caption below the picture says: *Laborers waiting for the third section of the labor train northward bound on the outskirts of Savannah, Georgia. The exodus of labor from the South has caused much alarm among the Southern whites, who have failed to treat them decent. The men, tired of being kicked and cursed, are leaving by the thousands as the above picture shows.*

1. What information do the photograph and caption give you?
2. How might African Americans living in other parts of the South have felt when they saw this picture and read the caption?

Case Study Review

Identifying Main Ideas

1. What tactics did Northern industrialists use to encourage Southern African Americans to move North?
2. What persuasive arguments did some African American leaders use to convince African Americans to remain in the South?
3. Why do you think the *Chicago Defender*, a Northern newspaper, appealed to so many African Americans in the South?

Working Together

Form a small group. Imagine that you work in the advertising department of a large Northern manufacturing company. Design an advertisement or poster that encourages African American workers to migrate North to work for your company.

Active Learning

Writing an Editorial Review the notes that you have taken while you read this case study. Use your notes to write an editorial for an African American newspaper being published during World War I. Begin by writing a main idea statement that identifies the topic and purpose of your editorial. List some facts and examples to support your position. Then write a first draft of your editorial. After you have reviewed your first draft, revise it and prepare a final copy.

Lessons for Today

In the 1900s, labor recruiters painted glowing pictures of life in the North, emphasizing high wages paid by northern companies. In response, many African American workers began a Great Migration in search of greater opportunities and a better life. Today, other things may appeal to African Americans in promising opportunities. One such source is the armed services. How do recruiters encourage African Americans and others to join the armed forces? How do their methods compare with those used by labor recruiters and the *Chicago Defender* in the 1900s? How is army life often portrayed in brochures and TV ads?

What Might You Have Done?

Imagine that you are a white Southerner greatly concerned about how many African American workers are migrating to the North. Write a letter to the governor of your state advising him what steps he could take to improve life for African Americans to convince them to stay in the South.

Analyzing Point of View

The Language of Thinking

Often a writer or speaker provides clues that signal a certain point of view. Look for "loaded" words and phrases that appeal to emotion rather than reason, personal beliefs, and value judgments. Consider also the type of information presented as well as information that was ignored.

You may have encountered people who held points of view that you thought were unfair or harmful to others. Point of view refers to how a speaker or writer presents an issue or event. By presenting one side of an issue, writers and speakers try to persuade people to think and act in a certain way.

Consider how white Southerners reacted to losing their workforce. Read the following section taken from an editorial that appeared in a Nashville, Tennessee, newspaper:

The Negroes who have gone North haven't gone because of any bad treatment accorded them here. They have gone because agents came South in search of labor and offered them higher wages than they were making here.

However, not all white Southerners blamed recruiters. Some realized that change was needed to keep African American laborers in the South. This point of view is reflected in the following editorial published in the Montgomery, Alabama, *Advertiser*:

The Negroes who are leaving the South in large numbers prefer to remain here. But they want something to eat and to wear. They want a brighter future held out to them. They want to be reasoned with by their landlords and want things made plain to them in the adjustment of yearly accounts [money paid to sharecroppers at the end of the year; landowners often didn't tell sharecroppers how much profit was made on the crops when they were sold]; they want to be protected against lynching and personal abuse; they want better treatment on the farms, on the common carriers [buses, trains], and in public places in general.

Think about the differing points of view reflected in the two editorials. Answer the following questions by using the information in the two editorial passages and information you have learned in the case study.

1. **Identifying Main Ideas** Who does the first editorial say is the cause of African Americans leaving the South?

2. **Analyzing** Does the point of view of the first editorial fit with what you have read in this case study? Explain your answer.

3. **Identifying Main Ideas** What changes does the second editorial suggest to convince African Americans to stay in the South?

4. **Synthesizing Information** Suppose that each of the editorial writers had exactly the same information about what was going on. Why do you think they had different points of view? Explain your answer.

Below is a Venn diagram. It is used to determine similarities and differences between two subjects. Copy the diagram into your notebook. In the overlapping part of the circles, write down all the things that each newspaper article had in common. In the parts that do not overlap, write down what was unique about each passage.

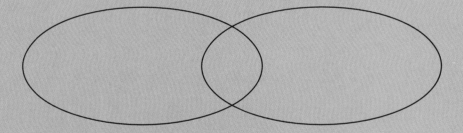

These travelers are waiting at a Southern train station. Sometimes officials would stop migrants and force them to turn back.

BOUND FOR THE PROMISED LAND

CRITICAL THINKING

- What factors influenced Southern-born African Americans' decisions to move North?
- What challenges did African Americans from rural areas face when they arrived in Northern cities?

TERMS TO KNOW

- migrants
- chain migration
- destination
- boycotts
- *de facto* segregation
- ghettos

ACTIVE LEARNING

A storyboard is a plan of action. It consists of a series of cartoons or sketches. When movie directors plan a scene, they first draw it on paper. Then everyone has an idea of what the scene will look like before it is filmed. After you read this case study, you will draw the storyboards for a film on the Great Migration. The Active Learning boxes in this case study will give you ideas for several storyboard panels.

On a sunny spring day in 1917, the Illinois Central train chugged across the Ohio River, which divides Kentucky from Indiana. The moment the train reached the other side, a great shout of joy rose up from the African Americans crowded into the "Colored Only" passenger car. They were no longer in the South!

Some of the passengers knelt in the aisles to pray, and many voices blended to sing the old spiritual, "I Done Come Out of the Land of Egypt, Ain't That Good News."

These travelers and many more who came before and after were **migrants**, people who move from one place to another. Many of these newcomers knew the Biblical story of the Israelites' flight from Egypt. So it was natural for them to compare their own situation with the one they had read about in the Bible. The Israelites had been kept in bondage in Egypt. These African American migrants had known bondage of a different kind in the South. The Israelites had fled from Egypt and, in time, arrived in Canaan, the land promised to them by the Lord. Now the African Americans had escaped from their old lives. They had traveled North and were bound for a Promised Land, where they thought their lives would be better.

Active Learning: For your first storyboard you might draw the scene in which migrants cross over the river. Draw one panel to show them reaching the North.

 # Making a Tough Decision

Migrants come from many backgrounds. When they move, they leave behind family, friends, and places that are familiar. They often face strange situations; they have to find jobs and housing, and they meet new people. For African American migrants in the early 1900s, moving meant crowded tenements, job lines, segregation, and discrimination.

The Security of Home

At first, most African Americans who migrated from the South were young males, who were healthy and able to do hard labor. As time passed, men and women of all ages, both farmers and city dwellers, moved northward. What they had in common was ambition and a strong desire to find a better life for themselves. They said good-bye to a familiar way of life and hello to an unfamiliar one. This decision was never easy.

Despite crop failures, low wages, and few jobs, most African Americans felt secure in the South. They loved the land and knew how to live on it. As Booker T. Washington, a respected African American leader in the early 1900s, said,

> [I have] never seen any part of the world where it seems to me the masses of the Negro people would be better off than right here in the southern states.

Family Ties

The decision to migrate involved entire families. Often, it was impossible to move everyone in the family at once. Instead, it was common to send one person ahead to find work and housing. Then, as money became available, other family members moved, until the entire family was reunited.

In many cases, whole communities followed this pattern, called **chain migration**. Chain migration is the process by which communities are joined together again as families and friends move to a new location.

Chain migration might work like this: Suppose three families agreed to journey to Chicago together. They arrived there and found housing near each other. They sent letters back to their friends that they were doing well, and several of their friends then decided to migrate, too. When these new migrants arrived in Chicago, they stayed with the first group of migrants. Soon others joined them, and the neighborhood filled with people from the same town in the South. The barber opened his shop down the street. The grocer opened a store around the corner. Within a few years, the new Chicago neighborhood became a copy of the migrants' Southern neighborhood.

Collecting enough money to pay for a trip North often required several years of work in the cotton fields.

Active Learning: A group of people migrating together tells a story. Draw two panels of the storyboard for this section. Draw one panel showing people getting ready to migrate. For the second panel, show migrants boarding a train.

Church and Community

Leaving the South also meant leaving one's church community. This was a significant loss because the church played a vital role in the lives of most African Americans. A church was the center of both religious life and social life for most Southern African Americans. Church was where people prayed, exchanged news, sang gospel music, kept up friendships, and offered support in times of need. Often, church was also a schoolhouse and a clubhouse for young African Americans.

Church ministers were highly respected members of their communities. These ministers attended meetings that brought Northern and Southern religious leaders together. In this way, ministers became an information link between family members who had been separated when some migrated North. They also provided news of job opportunities.

At first, some ministers discouraged their people from migrating. Still, African Americans continued to look to the North as the Promised Land. They turned away from the security of home and toward a future in a Northern city. At an African Methodist Episcopal conference in 1917, one minister reported losing more than half his members within six months. He said,

Bishop, I just come here to notify you that I'm getting ready to follow my flock.

In time, many ministers followed their congregations to Northern cities. There, the church again became the center of African American communities.

In the North, African American churches played a new and vital role in helping migrants. Many churches focused on meeting the survival needs of their members, such as helping them find housing and employment. Several churches also opened classrooms so that migrants could learn practical skills like cooking and sewing.

Thinking It Over

1. What was chain migration?
2. **Predicting Consequences** How might migrants' lives have been different if they had not had their churches as the center of their communities?

A Good CD to Listen to

The Essential Gospel Sampler. Columbia, Sony Music Entertainment, 1994.

On this CD, various African American artists sing classic gospel music, including "Swing Down Chariot," "Didn't It Rain," and "Will the Circle Be Unbroken."

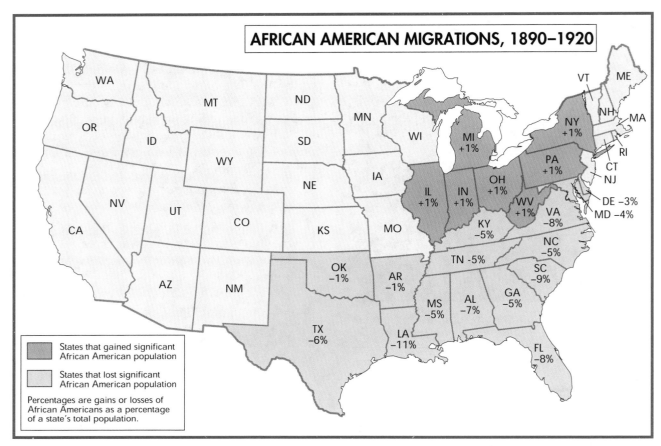

AFRICAN AMERICAN MIGRATIONS, 1890–1920

States that gained significant African American population

States that lost significant African American population

Percentages are gains or losses of African Americans as a percentage of a state's total population.

As this map shows, African American migration caused changes in the populations of many states. Which states lost population? Which states gained population?

2 The Journey North

For some people, glowing news about opportunities in the North added to their daily frustrations, and the attraction of the big cities caused them to act in haste. For those without families or ties to the community, a move could be made on the spur of the moment—like the story told below by a man who made his decision and just left:

> *I was plowing in the field and it was real hot. And I stayed with some of the boys who would leave home and [come] back . . . and would have money and clothes. I didn't have that. We all grew up together. And I said, Well, as long as I stay here I'm not goin' to get nowhere. And I tied that mule to a tree and caught a train.*

However, African Americans with families and responsibilities only moved after careful planning. Pulling up roots and leaving family members and friends behind was only part of the move. Migrants needed a place to go, a way to get there, and the money to pay for the trip. For most people, this was a long, well-planned process.

Choosing a Destination

A migrant's final **destination**, the place to which he or she went, was often determined by geography and transportation routes. With little money to spend, the quickest, cheapest, most direct route to a new job became the chosen route.

African Americans living in Mississippi or Louisiana, for example, often ended up in Chicago because the Illinois Central Railroad ran from New Orleans, Louisiana northward to Chicago. Those people living along the Eastern seaboard frequently traveled by ship to ports like Philadelphia, New York, and Boston.

Finding the Money

Paying for the journey was a major problem. Most farm families had only the income from their crops to feed, clothe, and house themselves.

Finding another source of income—a second job—was difficult. Farm communities had very little industry, so jobs were scarce. Some families solved the problem by making the move in small stages, going first to an industrial city in the South, saving their money, then using the savings for the last leg of the journey North.

While still in the South, young men sometimes worked in turpentine camps, sawmills, and cottonseed-oil mills to earn money. Young women could earn extra cash by washing, cooking, cleaning or through child care. These people returned to their farms during plowing, planting, and harvest seasons.

Hardships of Travel

Migrants traveled by every method available: train, ship, bus, car, and even on foot. The trip North was filled with hardships.

In the South, many white Southerners grew angry as large numbers of African Americans started to migrate northward. White land owners, who relied on African Americans to work in their fields for low wages, were very upset that their source of cheap labor was rapidly disappearing.

Migrating African Americans faced barriers to their travel even when they reached train or bus stations. Often, they were stopped from boarding trains or buses, and they were even arrested when trying to leave.

For example, in Brookhaven, Mississippi, a group of 200 African Americans was arrested while waiting on the platform for the next northbound train. Members of another group who were waiting

A Good Book to Read

Black Boy by Richard Wright. New York: The Library of America, Harper Perennial, 1991.

This reissue of Wright's autobiography reveals Wright's experiences in the North, which convinced him the Promised Land was nowhere to be found, either in the South or the North.

at the same train station had to leave their baggage behind. In order to board the train, they had to claim they were taking a day trip to visit relatives, and they had to have friends send their luggage to them in the North.

Once on board, African American travelers could not sit with whites. African Americans were forced to sit in train cars marked "Colored Only," usually located directly behind coal-burning engines. These cars were often filthy, had ragged seats, and no bathrooms. African Americans were prohibited by law from eating in the dining cars or buying tickets for sleeping compartments on trains. As a result, they often arrived in Northern cities hungry, dirty, and tired.

The segregation of the races in the South was due to the enforcement of "Jim Crow Laws." These laws separated African Americans from whites in all public places. African Americans were forced to sit in the rear of public buses and to travel in separate train cars. They had to use restrooms, water fountains, and restaurants labeled "colored."

These laws, so named because "Jim Crow" was a Southern nickname for African American people, extended to every aspect of public life, even doorways, prisons, stairways, and telephone booths. For example, in Florida, schools had separate facilities for storing text books for African Americans and for whites, and Georgia had two different Bibles for swearing in witnesses in court, one for whites and one for African Americans.

Migration Clubs

While songs like "Bound for the Promised Land" and "Northward Bound" lifted the spirits of migrating African Americans, what was really needed was an organized, practical approach to moving. This need led to new organizations—migration clubs. These clubs took advantage of group train rates and arranged group departure dates. Moving in a group provided security for individual migrants.

Usually, club organizers were influential people, such as ministers, labor agents, church deacons, and educators. But occasionally, club organization upset normal community leadership patterns. A large number of clubs were organized by women; this was surprising because most community leaders at the time were men.

Migration clubs furthered the concept of chain migration. Groups from a certain area of the South often headed for a particular destination in the North, thus reestablishing their community there.

The spirit behind migration clubs was strong, as one daughter of a sharecropper wrote:

> Some said good bye cheerfully . . . others fearfully, with terrors of unknown dangers in their mouths . . . others in the eagerness for distance said nothing. The daybreak found them gone. They said North. Trains said North. The tides and tongues said North and men moved like great herds before the glaciers.

Thinking It Over

1. What were Jim Crow Laws?
2. **Drawing Conclusions** How did Jim Crow laws affect African American travelers?

---

3 First Look at a New Life

By 1915, the first wave of the Great Migration was in full motion. Hundreds, and then thousands of African Americans poured into Northern cities, spurred on by ambition and the desire for a better life. Between 1900 and 1910, about 200,000 African Americans became migrants. That number grew to about 478,000 between 1910 and 1920.

Reaching Out a Helping Hand

For many African Americans, Northern city life was totally different from their lives on small Southern farms. Tall buildings, crowded streets, frigid winter weather, and the demand for skilled, rather than unskilled workers, overwhelmed migrants. Many migrants had skills required for farm work, but not the skills they needed for jobs in the North. In addition, they found themselves still surrounded by prejudice and segregated into run-down areas of major cities.

Fortunate newcomers were met by relatives or friends. Others were on their own, and with no connections, they had no idea where to find a place to stay or how to find a job. As musician Louis Armstrong later wrote when describing his arrival at Chicago's Illinois Central Railroad Station when he was young,

> I saw a million people. . . . I never seen a city that big. All those tall buildings. I said, no, this is the wrong city. I was fixing to take the next train back home. . . .

Sometimes, tricksters took advantage of new arrivals by cheating them out of their money or pulling them into criminal activities. As a result, a number of protective organizations were set up. In Chicago, for example, migrants were often met at the train by representatives of the Travelers' Aid Society. Members of the Travelers' Aid Society referred newcomers to the Urban League office for jobs or directed them to the local African American branch of the Young Men's Christian Association (YMCA) or the Young Women's Christian Association (YWCA) for a place to stay. In 1917, the Travelers' Aid Society hired its first African American assistants because migrants feared asking questions of white officials.

Other organizations sprang up throughout the country to help with the Great Migration. The Philadelphia Association for the Protection of Colored Women provided shelter for women newcomers. The YMCA, the YWCA, and the National Urban League, among others, helped

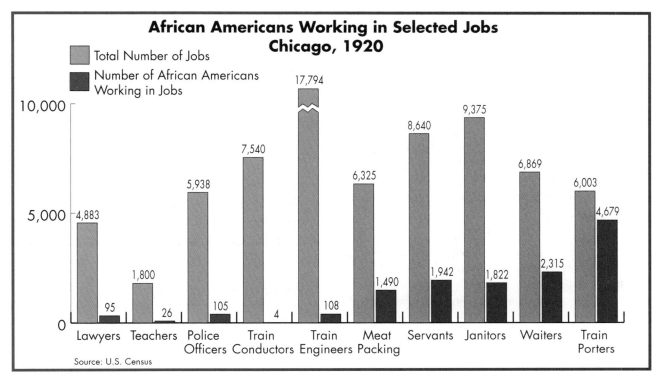

African Americans Working in Selected Jobs Chicago, 1920

Legend:
- Total Number of Jobs
- Number of African Americans Working in Jobs

Job	Total Number of Jobs	Number of African Americans Working in Jobs
Lawyers	4,883	95
Teachers	1,800	26
Police Officers	5,938	105
Train Conductors	7,540	4
Train Engineers	17,794	108
Meat Packing	6,325	1,490
Servants	8,640	1,942
Janitors	9,375	1,822
Waiters	6,869	2,315
Train Porters	6,003	4,679

Source: U.S. Census

African American migrants often found that better-paying jobs were not available to them.

newcomers locate housing, provided job information, and offered day-care facilities.

In Chicago, for example, the Urban League helped over 20,000 people find jobs and homes within a two-year period. They also offered industrial job training and conducted health and crime surveys in African American neighborhoods. The Urban League organized **boycotts** of businesses that would not hire African Americans. A boycott is a refusal to buy a product until particular demands are met.

A Good Book to Read

The Black Americans by Milton Meltzer. New York: Thomas Y. Crowell, 1964.

A history of African Americans told through letters, speeches, articles, and eyewitness accounts.

Regardless of ability, experience, or education, most African Americans worked in lower-paying, non-professional jobs. Many African American men could find jobs as waiters, porters, or janitors. But very few of them were allowed to work as teachers, train conductors, or police officers. Most African American women found that the jobs open to them were mainly as maids, cooks, and child-care workers.

De facto Segregation

Learning the ways of a Northern city was hard for many migrants. One of their first unfortunate lessons was that racial prejudice was not limited to the South.

Separation of the races existed in the North in fact, if not in law. This unwritten practice of keeping African Americans and whites separate is called *de facto* **segregation**.

De facto segregation affected housing opportunities for African Americans. White hostility forced African Americans to move into run-down neighborhoods, called **ghettos.** A ghetto is a section of a city where a minority or ethnic group lives due to social, economic, or legal pressure.

When a newcomer finally found housing, it was usually in an African American neighborhood. All big cities had such districts: the South Side in Chicago, Paradise Valley in Detroit, and Harlem in New York City were some examples.

Although public transportation was not segregated in the North, restaurants often refused to seat African Americans. In theaters, ushers led them to balcony seats. In department stores, clerks steered African Americans to the bargain basement. As Rebecca Taylor observed:

I discovered that Plainfield [a city in New Jersey] was as segregated as the South. It was almost the same, but the only thing I guess was you didn't have to sit in the back of the bus . . . But, everything else was just like it was down South. I didn't see any difference because the

---

SELF-HELP

1. Do not loaf. Get a job at once.
2. Do not live in crowded rooms. Others can be obtained.
3. Do not carry on loud conversations in street cars and public places.
4. Do not keep your children out of school.
5. Do not send for your family until you get a job.
6. Do not think you can hold your job unless you are industrious, sober, efficient and prompt.

   Cleanliness and fresh air are necessary for good health. In case of sickness send immediately for a good physician. Become an active member in some church as soon as you reach the city.

The Chicago Urban League distributed this list of ways to help African Americans from the rural South adjust to life in the urban North.

theaters were segregated, the hospitals were segregated, and, the churches, of course.

Active Learning: Imagine some specific situations in which a newcomer might experience racial prejudice in the North. Draw two storyboard panels for this section. The first should show a migrant looking for housing. The second can show newcomers looking for work, going to the "Colored Only" section of a movie theater, or worshipping in an all-African American church.

Old-settlers Against Newcomers

Most surprising to Southern-born migrants was the disapproval of Northern-born African Americans. Many long-established residents felt that the behavior and country customs of the poorer and less educated newcomers reflected badly on all people of color. Newspapers, like Chicago's *Defender,* and organizations, such as the National Urban League, started advertising campaigns to teach migrants the ways of city life.

"Old-settlers," as long-time Northern African Americans were known, encouraged and assisted migrants basically from self-interest. To politicians, the newcomers were voters. To businessmen, they were customers. Fearing a negative impression on the white community, they had reason to help newcomers adjust to city life and customs. African American migrants who became involved in crime or followed rural customs reflected badly on the African American community as a whole. Claimed the *Defender,* "We are our brother's keeper, whether we like it or not."

Daily life for migrant African Americans created deep racial tensions. Northern whites were openly hostile; Northern African Americans too often voiced their disapproval. Newspapers such as the *Defender* spoke out against the habits of some Southern-born African Americans. One article stated:

Keep your mouth shut, please! There is entirely too much loud talking on the streetcars among our newcomers . . .

The Red Summer

Once World War I was over and white soldiers began to return home, jobs for African Americans became scarce. With high unemployment, overcrowded tenement housing, plus higher-than-average illness and death rates, many cities were ready to explode into violence.

In the summer of 1919, called the Red Summer by author James Weldon Johnson, there were about 25 race riots. Some were large; others small; all showed the negative state of race relations. Race riots were not limited to any one region, to a city of any particular size, or even to the North or South.

Perhaps the worst riot took place in Chicago. It began over a disagreement on a Lake Michigan beach. A young African American swam in an area that was usually used only by whites. The white swimmers demanded that the young man leave, and some threw stones at him. When the man sank and drowned, African Americans said that he had been murdered. Rumors flew throughout the city; mobs formed, and fighting exploded all over Chicago.

The riots lasted two weeks, and the militia was called to keep order. When the riots ended, at least 38 people had been killed and over 500 others injured. More than 1,000 families were left homeless due to fires set during the fighting.

The riots of the Red Summer did not change the way of life for African American migrants in the North. Segregation in its several forms continued. Violence had not solved anything. There were many for whom violence was not the answer. For example, the Commission on Interracial Cooperation was organized in 1919. Its goal was to calm racial tensions "which were flaming at the time with such deadly menace in all sections of the country."

Another organization, the National Association for the Advancement of Colored People (NAACP), begun in 1909, worked to prevent violence against African Americans. It also fought against the root causes of violence—unjust legal penalties and discrimination. For example, African Americans arrested during the Washington, D.C. riots received much harsher jail sentences than did whites arrested at the same

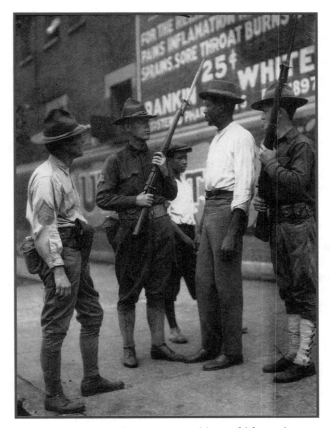

The Chicago riot of 1919 caused loss of life and property. Here, soldiers question an African American during the riot.

time. Lawyers for the NAACP protested against that injustice.

These organizations and others spoke out against injustice and promoted a positive image of African Americans migrants and their contributions to urban communities. They promoted the idea that violence was not the solution to racial problems.

Thinking It Over

1. What factors caused race riots during the Red Summer?
2. **Analyzing** Why do you think Northern African Americans disapproved of Southern African American migrants?

GOING TO THE SOURCE

A First Glimpse of Chicago

The African American author Richard Wright was born and raised in Mississippi. His grandparents had been enslaved. His father was a poor cotton farmer, and his mother was a schoolteacher. In 1927, when he was 19, Wright and his aunt moved to Chicago. In his autobiography, *Black Boy,* he recalls his first impressions of the city:

My first glimpse of the flat black stretches of Chicago depressed and dismayed me, mocked all my fantasies. Chicago seemed an unreal city whose mythical houses were built of slabs of black coal wreathed in . . . gray smoke, houses whose foundations were sinking slowly into the dank prairie. Flashes of steam showed . . . on the wide horizon, gleaming . . . in the winter sun. The din [noise] of the city entered my consciousness, entered to remain for years to come. The year was 1927.

What would happen to me here? Would I survive? My expectations were modest. I wanted only a job . . .

The train rolled into the depot. Aunt Maggie and I got off and walked slowly through the crowds into the station. I looked about to see if there were signs saying: FOR WHITE—FOR COLORED. I saw none. Black people and white people moved about, each seemingly intent upon his private mission. There was no racial fear. Indeed, each person acted as though no one existed but himself. It was strange to pause before a crowded newsstand without having to wait until a white man was served. And yet, because everything was so new, I began to grow tense again, although it was a different sort of tension than I had known before. I knew that this machine city was governed by strange laws, and I wondered if I would ever learn them.

1. Was Wright's first impression of Chicago positive or negative? Use quotes from the selection to support your ideas.

2. **Drawing Conclusions** Lifestyles in Chicago were different from what Wright was used to in the South. How do you know this is true?

Case Study Review

Identifying Main Ideas

1. Why was the decision to migrate to the North such a difficult one for many African Americans to make?
2. What different factors did migrants have to consider when planning their journeys?
3. What problems did newcomers face as they tried to fit in to Northern city life?

Working Together

Work in a group to plan a "migration" from where you live today to another region of the United States or another country. Decide where your group will go, how you will get there, what things about your current life you want to keep, what things you want to change, and what you hope will happen when you arrive at your new location. Consider the problems you might have as a group migrating to this new place. Write your ideas in a short essay to be read to the class.

 ### Active Learning

Creating a Storyboard Put together the storyboard scenes that you created as you read this case study. Use them to create a final presentation for your film on the Great Migration. Review your storyboard. Add other illustrations if you like. Then write a brief narration that links all the scenes. Present your storyboards to the class, reading the narration aloud.

Lessons for Today

The National Urban League, founded in 1910, trained migrants for industrial work and helped them settle into city life. During the early years of migration, thousands of migrants were helped in their efforts to find housing, jobs, and training they needed to survive. Today, the National Urban League remains an active organization, dedicated to improving economic and social opportunities for African Americans. What areas should the Urban League focus on in today's society to help African Americans advance?

What Might You Have Done?

It's 1919. You are in an area of Chicago where rioting is going on. You see a mob set fire to a house. What would you do? Should you take action? If so, what action? Why might you choose to not do anything?

The Language of Thinking

There is more to what writers say than just the words on the page. By careful reading you can discover whether the writer is a man or woman, old or young, happy or angry. You can sometimes determine facts about a writer's background: education, religious influences, and political influences.

When you add up the facts and draw a conclusion from the information, this is called making an inference, or "reading between the lines."

Critical readers pay careful attention to the kinds of information a writer presents. They learn to distinguish facts from opinions, and they look beyond what the words say to find deeper meanings.

The letter below was written to the editor of Chicago's *Defender*, an African American newspaper. As you read, think about what you learn about the writer.

Miami, Fla., May 4, 1917

Dear Sir: Some time ago down this side it was a rumour about the great work going on in the north. But at the present time every thing is quiet there, people saying that all we have been hearing was false. Until I caught hold of the Chicago Defender. *I see where its more positions are still open. Now I am very anxious to get up there. I follows up cooking. I also was a stevedor. I used to have from 150 to 200 men under my charge. They thought I was capable in doing the work and at the meantime I am willing to do anything. I have a wife and she is a very good cook. She has lots of references from the north and south. Now dear sir if you can send me a ticket so I can come up there and after I get straightened out I will send for my wife. You will oblige me by doing so at as early date as possible.*

1. **Understanding Text** Do you think this man had a job when he wrote the letter? Explain your answer.

2. **Interpreting** What does this man's use of language tell us about him? Note the words he chooses and how he explains his situation.

3. **Making Inferences** What ideas does this man have about migrating to the North? How do you know?

4. **Making Inferences** Is this man a responsible worker? How do you know?

Seeking a better life, these African Americans loaded their belongings and headed North.

GETTING AHEAD

CRITICAL QUESTIONS

■ How was factory labor in the North different from farm work in the South?

■ How did Northern churches, schools, and organizations help African American migrants adapt to life in the North?

TERMS TO KNOW

■ productivity
■ strikebreakers
■ domestic servants
■ entrepreneurs
■ discrimination

ACTIVE LEARNING

After you read this case study, you will write a letter from the point of view of an African American who has arrived in a Northern city between 1916 and 1920. This letter will be directed to family members who have remained in the South. In it, you will describe your new life in the city. As you read the case study, take notes on material you can use in your letter.

Factory smokestacks belching soot and grime, staining clothes . . . clogging lungs . . . Shabby old houses carved into dozens of small, cramped apartments. . .

These were among Lilly McKnight's first impressions of life in a Northern city. When she arrived in Philadelphia from her small, rural town, she found a job in a garment factory. All day long, she pressed clothes—shirt after shirt, dress after dress.

After her day's work at the factory, McKnight returned to her tiny apartment. Little more than one room with bare furnishings, a small gas stove, and a sink, this apartment was once a bedroom in a seven-room apartment. The landlord had divided the larger apartment into five smaller ones that shared one central bathroom.

Rent for McKnight's one small room was about $30 per month. The landlord, who had charged $50 per month for the one large apartment, now collected more than $30 per month for each of the five smaller apartments—more than $150 each month!

Thoughts of her children, who had been left behind with her sister's family, filled McKnight's mind. This bare room was not her dream. This work was not for her. Years later, she recalled,

> *It just didn't suit me . . . You want to be satisfied in what you do. If you aren't, then you want to do somein' else, right?*

1 Making Ends Meet

Like Lilly McKnight, many African American migrants who came to the North sought better-paying jobs. Their new work, like their new lives, was vastly different from their familiar routines of the South.

New Opportunities

Although the jobs that were available differed from city to city, most opportunities for African Americans involved brooms, shovels, or tools. Farm life had not prepared African Americans with the kind of skills that enabled them to practice trades in the North. Manual labor, which required no specific skills or education, seemed to be the destiny for many African Americans.

Detroit's economy revolved around automobile manufacturing. In Chicago, it was slaughterhouses and meatpacking plants. In Pittsburgh, jobs were found in steel mills. Other available jobs were also on low-paying levels—porters, waiters, and laborers.

Only New York provided a wide variety of jobs, from longshoremen on the docks to the

Many migrants found work in unskilled jobs that paid low wages and offered no advancement.

garment industry. James Weldon Johnson said of New York's job market,

> *I think there is less danger to the Negroes of New York of losing out economically and industrially than to the Negroes of any large city in the North. In most of the big industrial centers Negroes are engaged in gang labor [large groups employed together in one industry]. . . . Employment among Negroes in New York is highly diversified . . . So the danger of great numbers of Negroes being thrown out of work at once, with a resulting economic crisis among them, is less in New York.*

New Work Rules

In the rural South, there were two seasons during which people labored from sunrise to sundown: spring planting and fall harvesting. Winter and summer were spent trying to find other work to put food on the table. At the end of the year, a farmer's success was measured by the size of his crop. **Productivity**, the amount of output per worker, could be measured by the rows of tobacco planted in a day or the amount of cotton picked per day.

In the North, workers had to "clock in" by punching a time clock to let the boss know what time they started and finished work. Being ten minutes late meant the loss of an hour's pay. Being on time was important, particularly in assembly-line jobs, where one late employee held up other workers on the line.

A Good Book to Read

12 Million Black Voices, text by Richard Wright; photo direction by Edwin Rosskam. New York: Thunders Mouth Press, 1992.

This book, originally published in 1942, offers nearly 150 black-and-white scenes dramatizing the lives of African Americans: rural poverty, urban weariness, and the spiritual comfort received from the church.

African Americans took many kinds of jobs in the North. These men tightened rivets in the Hudson River tunnel connecting New York and New Jersey.

Productivity for Northern factory workers was also measured by how much product a worker turned out. In the garment industry, workers were measured by the number of pieces they completed. On assembly lines, it could be the number of bolts tightened or the tons of steel produced.

The differences between the two work styles were significant. Farm workers had longer hours during peak seasons, and pay was based on the size of their crop at the end of the harvest. They did not have to punch a time clock every single day or work at a pace set by others.

Many former farm workers, both white and African American, found factory work demanding. Not only were their jobs dependent on being on time, but they also had short meal and rest breaks, as well as a quick work pace.

In an automobile plant, for example, cars moved slowly on rails through the work place. When a car stopped at a particular work station, the laborer only had a certain amount of time to perform a specific task, such as spray-painting the body, installing windows, or putting on tires. Then the car moved on and another took its place. Workers performed the same task hundreds of times a day—and hundreds of times the next day—and the day after that.

The pace of work was set by the assembly line. If a manager needed to produce more cars, he increased the speed of the line. Workers who couldn't keep pace were usually fired.

In meatpacking plants, a worker became just one part in the process. A man who used to butcher a whole hog now only made one or two cuts on a hog carcass, then performed the same task on the next piece as it came by him on hooks.

It was hard to feel pride in doing what many African Americans felt were "pieces of work." However, the pay was very good, compared to wages paid in the South. As one man in East Chicago wrote to his friend,

> *Now it is true that the colored men are making good. Never pay less than $3.00 per day for (10) hours—this is not promise. I do not see how they pay such wages the way they work labors. They do not hurry or drive you. . . .*

In 1916, daily wages in Chicago started at $2.00–$2.50 per day or about 25¢ per hour. By 1919, the average wage was 48¢ per hour, or almost $5.00 per day. This amounted to about $1,500 per year—a shockingly high wage compared to Southern farm incomes that were in the $100 to $300 dollars per year range.

Active Learning: For your letter home, imagine you have gotten a job in either a meatpacking or automotive plant. Take notes on what these jobs required, including both the positive and negative aspects of these jobs.

Women's Work

During World War I, because of the labor shortage, a number of factory jobs opened up for African American women. When the war ended and white soldiers returned to civilian life, these jobs became scarce. Then both African American women and men struggled to find work.

Prejudice against African Americans and against women limited opportunities for female migrants. Many migrant women who worked outside their homes found employment as domestic servants, cooks, and laundry workers.

Women in the North, as in the South, were limited to such jobs as cooks, nannies, laundresses, and **domestic servants**. A domestic servant is someone who works in a private home, such as a maid or cleaning woman.

It was possible for domestic servants to earn as much or more than factory workers. Lilly McKnight became a domestic servant after she left her job in the garment industry. With the money she earned in her new job, she was finally able to bring her children to Philadelphia.

Hours for domestic work were long— between 12 and 14 hours per day, and longer at an employer's request. Women's wages averaged $12 to $18 per week for factory work in Chicago; domestic servants were paid a comparable wage, plus their room and board.

Despite some advantages to domestic work, many African American women were against resuming what they considered to be the master-servant relationship that existed before the Civil War. Said one migrant who chose working in a box factory to domestic work,

> I'll never work in nobody's kitchen but my own any more. No indeed! That's the one that makes me stick to this job. You do have some time to call your own.

Thinking It Over

1. How was the pace of work in the North different from the pace in the South?
2. **Drawing Conclusions** What disadvantages were connected with assembly-line work?

2 Fighting the Job Ceiling

Most migrants found that they were considerably better off up North than they had been in the South. Wages were two and three times higher than they had been in the South for similar jobs. Although housing and food cost more, there was also more variety in entertainment and the chance for an education.

Nevertheless, job opportunities were limited by several factors. Lack of education and skilled training limited the types of jobs open to African Americans. At the same time, many migrants faced **discrimination** in many work situations.

Some migrants went into business for themselves. This African American-owned company moved migrants from one part of Cleveland, Ohio to another part.

Discrimination means treating someone in a different way based on the person's race, religion, sex, family background, or social status.

No Place for Advancement

Nine out of ten African American factory employees worked as common laborers, sweeping, cleaning, and carrying loads. There was little opportunity to train for a higher position or to learn special skills that could lead to better jobs.

No matter how the labor market changed, African American workers were unable to rise above the "job ceiling," an invisible barrier that kept African Americans in unskilled or semi-skilled jobs. As late as 1930 in Chicago, 75 percent of African American men and 90 percent of the women were still below the job ceiling.

During World War I, when recruiters toured the South looking for laborers, jobs were plentiful. As one migrant in Pittsburgh said,

> Some of the mills would need labor so bad, they'd have a man sometimes right at the mill. When you'd pass on the street, he'd inform you . . . he was going to hire so and so many today. And you could go in and be interviewed and you may get a job. It was very easy—very easy to get a job.

However, racial tension still existed and many whites feared that the rush of African American migrants would flood the labor market and deprive them of jobs. For example, in East St. Louis, Illinois, a labor dispute arose in May 1917, and quickly erupted into a riot. Armed white mobs prowled the streets, attacked African Americans, and tried to force them from the city. By the end of the violence, 39 residents had been killed, hundreds injured, and thousands driven from their homes.

After the war, there were more people looking for jobs than there were jobs available. Competition was fierce, even for low-level positions. Men lined up along the outside of factory walls, hoping to be picked for a day's labor, or, even better, a permanent job.

Tensions boiled and frequently erupted in violence. During the summer of 1919, called the Red Summer, riots broke out in cities all across the nation.

Active Learning: Take notes on the labor situation for use in your letter home.

Organized Labor

As African Americans sought higher-paying positions and more profitable skills, they met with a force that was sometimes friend, sometimes foe—organized labor. Unions were slow to accept African Americans as members. Many white laborers believed African Americans were strongly anti-union, which helped Northern management keep the two work forces divided.

Although some unions actively discouraged African American members, most simply never made an effort to include the African American labor force. Unions tended to organize only skilled laborers, such as electricians, plumbers, and carpenters—and few African Americans had those skills. Only the United Mine Workers (UMW) and the Industrial Workers of the World (IWW) showed interest in organizing unskilled labor.

The few African American union members didn't always fare well. For example, Richard Davis, an African American member of the UMW, was unjustly accused by white union members of illegally organizing a strike. Although the UMW *Journal* supported Davis, he was unable to get work and felt unfairly treated. He wrote,

> I have as yet never boasted of what I have done in the interest of organized labor, but will venture to say that I have done all I could and am proud that I am alive today, for I think I have had the unpleasant privilege of going into the most dangerous places in this country to organize, or in other words, to do the almost impossible. I have been threatened; I have been sandbagged; I have been stoned, and last of all, deprived of the right to earn a livelihood for myself and family.

The largest national association of labor, called the American Federation of Labor (AFL), served as a "parent" union for smaller unions. The AFL had considerable influence in hiring decisions in union-dominated industries. Because they favored white members over African American nonmembers in hiring situations, AFL-organized trades had few African American employees.

In some situations, resentment built up between African American workers and union members. The white unionists believed that African Americans were **strikebreakers**, workers hired specifically to break a strike.

In many cases, African Americans were not aware they were being hired to break strikes. When they realized the situation, many quit the jobs, while others felt they had no choice but to take jobs that were available only because of the strike.

After World War I, unions began to organize less by skill than by industry. As unions developed in the steel, auto, and meatpacking industries, African Americans became valued union members. Union management came to realize that African Americans were a solid, growing labor force, and acceptance of African Americans became common.

Perhaps the most significant union breakthrough for African Americans was A. Philip Randolph's organization of an all-African American union—the Brotherhood of Sleeping Car Porters. It took many years for Randolph to convince railroad porters and maids to form a union to represent their interests.

In a long struggle against the Pullman company, the owner of railway sleeping cars, the Brotherhood won minor battles in the late 1920s, and it was fully recognized in 1937. The Brotherhood was the first African American union to receive a full charter by the AFL, the organization that 30 years before had refused membership to African American workers.

Not many African Americans were hired to work as railroad engineers or conductors. But thousands were porters on trains. When porters organized into a union, it proved to be a powerful force against the Pullman Company.

Thinking It Over

1. What caused riots in 1917 and 1919?
2. **Making Inferences** Why do you think unions began accepting African American members?

Active Learning: Be prepared to include news about unions in your letter home. Take notes on unions. Do the workers at your job belong to a union? If so, how does this affect you?

3 Rising to the Top

Despite the obstacles to success, some African Americans were able to make their way in the North and turn their skills, knowledge, and talents into financial successes. These migrants were **entrepreneurs** who recognized business needs in their communities. An entrepreneur is a person who starts and manages his or her own business. Once entrepreneurs recognized what people needed, they wisely turned those needs into opportunities through hard work.

A Solid Middle Class

The National Negro Business League recorded that the total number of African American business enterprises doubled from 20,000 in 1900 to 40,000 in 1914. The largest growth occurred among retail merchants—from 10,000 in 1900 to 25,000 in 1914.

While many African Americans made fortunes in real estate, most began service-oriented businesses, like barber shops, restaurants, newspapers, funeral homes, banks, and insurance companies. In 1918, Mississippi-born migrant William J. Lathan founded the Underwriter's Insurance Company, hiring fellow migrants to sell policies for him.

Another such entrepreneur was "Pig Foot Mary" Harris who turned her Southern-style cooking into a fortune. With only $5.00, Harris invested in a boiler, a baby carriage, and $2 worth of pigs' feet. She sold her cooking on the Harlem streets from the baby carriage. In just over a dozen years, Pig Foot Mary's "traveling restaurant" made her one of the wealthiest women in Harlem.

A Good Book to Read

Madam C. J. Walker: Self-Made Millionaire by Patricia and Frederick McKissack. Hillside, New Jersey: Enslow Publishers, 1992.

This is the story of a migrant who ventured into the business world with only $1.50 in her pocket and a recipe for a haircare product. By 1915, Ms. Walker had more than 15,000 representatives selling her products.

Perhaps the most fabulous rags-to-riches story was the rise of Madame C. J. Walker. An orphaned child of ex-slave sharecroppers, Walker worked as a laundress. Because of her poor diet and the demands of her work, Walker's hair began falling out.

According to legend, she "dreamed" about a recipe to combat baldness. Using $1.50, she started a hair-straightening empire, selling "Madame Walker's Wonderful Hair Grower." At her death,

African American businesses that offered services to their communities, such as barbershops, flourished in the North.

Walker was worth more than $2 million, and the sharecropper's daughter lived in a mansion in uptown New York City.

Professionals

The rise of African Americans in professions occurred as larger African American communities developed. These communities needed teachers for their schools; doctors, dentists, pharmacists, and nurses for better health care; attorneys and politicians; social workers; and ministers.

The African American professional class developed immediately after World War I and continued to grow as African American communities grew. Professionals played important roles as community leaders in addition to providing their services. For example, Dr. George Cleveland Hall, a Chicago doctor, was also an official in the National Association for the Advancement of Colored People (NAACP), as well as in the Washingtonian National Negro Business League, and a founder of the Chicago Urban League.

Thinking It Over

1. How did many African American entrepreneurs meet the demands of their communities?
2. **Analyzing** What roadblocks did African American entrepreneurs face in becoming successful?

---

4 Beyond the Work Place

To find relief from work-related stress, newcomers to the North sought out meaningful and satisfying activities within their communities. As in the South, the church played an important role. Education, unavailable to many African Americans in the South, became important during their free time, as did a variety of organizations. Surprisingly, many afterwork activities were work-related.

A Good Book to Read

Go Tell It on the Mountain by James Baldwin. New York: Modern Library, 1995.

This novel mirrors the author's own childhood and relationship to his church.

The Church Fills a Gap

Many migrants found their churches to be a source of help when it came to finding and keeping jobs. Arriving in the North, a migrant family might make church its first stop. Churches provided job listings, housing lists, and day-care facilities for working mothers. Churches also offered classes to train migrants for various jobs.

Due to its long-term relationship with many major employers, churches also played an important role as the go-between for employers looking for strikebreakers. This was a mutual relationship between big business and churches. In 1916, one minister in South Side Chicago recruited 300 African American women to break a strike by hotel maids, while another minister regularly arranged for strikebreakers to replace seamstresses of the International Ladies Garment Workers Union (ILGWU).

In return for support in supplying migrants who would work in their factories, African American churches in Chicago, for example, received financial support from white tycoons like Philip Armour, Cyrus McCormick, and Gustavus Swift. In fact, during a period in which many African Americans found themselves out of jobs, Swift assisted in Trinity Church's relief drive.

For the most part, African American ministers followed the lead of African Methodist Episcopal Bishop A. J. Carey, who said,

The interest of my people lies with the wealth of the nation and with the class of white people who control it.

Successful African American businessowners often hired other African Americans. These children, who sold newspapers on the streets of Cleveland, Ohio, worked for William O. Walker, an African American newspaper publisher.

Getting an Education

One important reason that many migrants moved North was the possibility of getting a better education both for their children and themselves. Migrants hoped that by acquiring the skills a good school taught, they would have better chances of finding better jobs.

Initially, African American students struggled in Northern schools. Although younger students adjusted well, their older brothers and sisters did not have a strong background in reading, writing, and mathematics. In the South, these students did not attend school regularly or they attended schools that were so overcrowded that learning was nearly impossible. With such a poor educational background, older students were often put in lower-level classes, teased for their lack of education, and considered less able to learn by white teachers.

However, Northern schools were the means to gain needed skills and provided an education that was superior to that provided by schools in the South. In Chicago, for example, few migrants could

find fault with the schools available for their children.

The oldest school in South Side, Moseley Elementary, while old, had cafeteria facilities, a gym, and manual training tools. The school had large classes, with about 40 students to one teacher. However, compared to Mississippi, where one class could have as many as 125 students to one teacher, the Chicago school was much preferred.

Adult education was also available at schools such as Chicago's Wendell Phillips High School. Adults could enroll in any elementary grade for one dollar and in high school for two dollars. These fees were refunded if the adult attended 75 percent of the classes. By 1921, nearly 4,000 African Americans were enrolled in Chicago's evening school.

Few migrants could argue with the Chicago *Defender's* reminder that "Education will force open the door of hope behind which is SUCCESS." By 1920, almost every African American child between six and thirteen attended school. More importantly, nearly twice as many African American students graduated from Northern high schools as graduated from Southern ones.

Joining in Community Life

In addition to church and school, many African American migrants joined organizations that helped them to make new friendships and give back to the communities in which they lived. Many migrants, having received the assistance of groups such as the YMCA and the Urban League, helped other migrants by participating in these organizations. Political groups, such as the Julia Ward Howe State Republican Club of Providence, Rhode Island, were popular as African American migrants exercised their right to vote and to hold political office.

In the North, as in the South, fraternal clubs or lodges provided important business and social connections, as well as political support. Robert R. Jackson, an Illinois politician, belonged to about 25 fraternal groups. The Masons, Elks, and Odd Fellows actively supported African American migrants by helping them find friends and offering a sense of belonging.

An Active Life

With 48-to 60-hour workweeks, church, school, and clubs, African American migrants soon settled into their new lives in the North. Despite its many hardships, life in the North was far better than what most migrants had known in the South. A strong sense of community and belonging added a sense of familiarity to a lifestyle that had seemed so strange to migrants on their arrival only a few years earlier.

Thinking It Over

1. What role did the church play in the employment of African Americans?
2. **Drawing Conclusions** Why do you think African American migrants valued adult education?

GOING TO THE SOURCE

What the Census Shows

The U.S. Census, taken every ten years, is an official count of the population. The table below is part of the census taken in 1920. It shows how African American women in Chicago were employed in various occupations at that time. Study the table and answer the questions below.

Occupation	Total Number of Jobs	Percentage of Jobs Held by African American Women
Dressmaker, seamstress	8,513	12.6
Store clerk	13,330	3.9
Actress (professional)	1,028	6.3
Teacher (professional)	11,739	1.2
Nurse (professional)	5,004	2.3
Barber, hairdresser	2,156	33.8
Housekeeper	4,982	6.4
Laundress (home)	6,638	43.0
Laundry operator	3,907	36.1
Servant	26,184	23.9
Waitress	5,175	13.1

Source: U.S. Census, 1920

1. In which three jobs were African American women employed the most?

2. In which three jobs were African American women employed the least?

3. **Interpreting the Table** What percentage of the teaching jobs in Chicago were held by African American women?

4. **Analysis** Review the list of "professional jobs" included in the census. What does this list tell you about professional opportunities for African American women in 1920?

Case Study Review

Identifying Main Ideas

1. What types of jobs were open to African American migrants coming to the cities?

2. Why did many African American workers find it difficult to get ahead in the North?

3. Why did migrants from the South create their own communities in Northern cities?

Working Together

Form a small group with three or four other students. Imagine that you are entrepreneurs who want to start a new business in a Northern African American community. Together, choose a product or service and a target market (the people you will sell to). Work together to write a business plan to submit to a bank for a small business loan. In your plan, describe the business and why you think it will be profitable. Identify the resources you need to get started and how you plan to use the money you borrow.

Active Learning

Writing a Letter Review the notes you took as you read this case study. Add other details you want to include in your letter. Think about the tone you want to set—upbeat, angry, funny, or matter-of-fact. Think also about any message that you want to send. For example, do you want to encourage or discourage family members from migrating North? Next, draft an outline to follow so that your letter is organized and your thoughts are easy to follow. Finally, think of an informal way to close your letter as you write.

Lessons for Today

The Young Negroes' Progressive Association of Detroit passed out cards to help migrants adjust to their new work situations. Like poems, these cards set out in verse the importance of getting to work on time, learning from mistakes, and not asking too many questions or falling behind. What behaviors and attitudes do you think are essential for success in today's work world? List them on a card you might distribute to job applicants.

What Might You Have Done?

Imagine that you and your family are longtime members of a Northern African American church. In the past year, several Southern migrant families have joined your church. What might you and your family do to help these new members cope with the pressures of city life?

Understanding Rationalizations and Justifications

The Language of Thinking

Many people use language to **rationalize** or **justify** their actions. A rationalization is an attempt to explain why one thinks or acts as he or she does; it is a way of reasoning. A justification is an attempt to show why someone is right or fair in thinking as he or she does. By using rationalizations and justifications, people can shift the blame for their actions to others.

When the AFL was first organized, Booker T. Washington and some other African American leaders complained that unions would not allow African Americans to become members. The AFL Executive Council defended its actions with the following statement:

The real difficulty in the matter is that the colored workers have allowed themselves to be used with too frequently telling [very effective] effect by their employers as to injure the cause and interests of themselves as well as white workers. They have too often allowed themselves to be regarded as "cheap men," and all realize that "cheap men" are not only an impediment [barrier] to the attainment [reaching] of the worker's just right, and the progress of civilization, but will tie themselves to the slough [swamp] of despond and despair. The antipathy [dislike] that we know some union workers have against the colored man is not because of this color, but because of the fact that generally he is a "cheap man." It is the constant aim of our movement to relieve all workers, white and black from such an unprofitable and unenviable [not desired] condition.

1. **Understanding the Document** How do union officials justify excluding African Americans from their union?

2. **Interpreting** Do the officials voice their own opinions or what they think are opinions of others? Why do they do this?

3. **Analysis** What is the tone of this passage? How does this tone help the union rationalize its position?

4. **Drawing Conclusions** Do you think the union will allow African Americans to become members? Explain your answer.

By carrying picket signs and sign boards, these people are protesting lynching. Lynching was one of the main targets of the NAACP.

THE FIGHT FOR JUSTICE

CRITICAL QUESTIONS

■ Why did African Americans have to fight for justice?

■ What victories did African Americans achieve in pursuit of equality?

TERMS TO KNOW

■ Talented Tenth

■ Bolshevist

■ biracial

ACTIVE LEARNING

After you read this case study, you will write a newspaper article on the founding of the NAACP. As you read this case study, take notes to help you write an article that answers each of the "five Ws" — who, what, when, where, and why.

By the early 1900s, Springfield, Illinois, was growing into a large industrial center. Springfield had the largest percentage of African American residents of any city in Illinois, most of whom were segregated in a section of the city. Many of the new Springfield residents were African American migrants. As the African American migrant population grew, competition for jobs grew fierce between the established white population and the migrants from Southern states.

In the summer of 1908, tempers flared due to several seemingly unrelated incidents. In July, an engineer named Clergy Ballard was murdered by Joe James, an African American. A few weeks later, Mabel Hallam, a white woman, claimed an African American handyman had assaulted her in her home.

After both men were arrested, an angry crowd of white men formed on the street outside the jail. Threats against the two men forced the sheriff, Charles Werner, to take them out of Springfield to prevent a lynching. The furious mob went into the African American section of town and attacked the local barbershop, which was owned by Scott Burton, an African American businessman. Burton fired his shotgun in the air to warn the crowd to stay away. The mob rushed Burton, killed him, and hanged him from a tree.

Then the mob moved into the African American residential area of Springfield, setting houses afire and forcing both migrant and longtime Springfield African American families to flee for their lives. The Illinois governor called out the National Guard to restore order. With the National Guard on patrol, Springfield seemed peaceful for awhile.

The next day, however, the angry white mob gathered in front of the old court house building. The people marched toward the state arsenal, where many African American migrants, homeless because of the fires, were living. The National Guard kept the mob from reaching the arsenal.

Enraged over being stopped by the National Guard, the crowd marched toward the home of William Donnegan. Donnegan was 84 years old and a longtime African American resident of Springfield. He was well-known for his financial support of African American migrants from the South, a fact which infuriated the uncontrollable white mob. Although he'd never been accused of any crime, the mob assaulted Donnegan, slitting his throat and lynching him in a nearby schoolyard. The National Guard cut him down, but it was too late. Donnegan died the following morning.

The news of the Springfield riot swept across the nation. Many people were outraged that Springfield, the home of Abraham Lincoln, had become the site of racial hatred. Political and social leaders called for swift justice. A special grand jury met and handed down 107 criminal charges against whites in Springfield. Yet only one person was actually convicted. When the trials were over, Mabel Hallam admitted that she had lied about being assaulted. The source of outrage for so many Springfield residents turned out to have been based on a falsehood.

Active Learning: The Springfield riot led to the formation of the NAACP. Take notes about the riot to use in your news article.

1 In Pursuit of Equality

The incident in Springfield was not an isolated event. For example, in Philadelphia, enraged whites dragged African Americans from streetcars, beat them, and threatened to kill them. The City Council of Syracuse, Ohio, banned African Americans from settling within the city's borders, as did several towns in Indiana. In 1906, a young African American in Greensburg, Indiana, was accused of assaulting his employer. The mob that gathered to lynch the young man did not succeed. However, the mob attacked the African American section of Greensburg, burning buildings, destroying property, and beating African American migrants.

Working Within the System

In spite of violence against African Americans, it was the hope of people like Booker T. Washington and W. E. B. DuBois that progress toward equality and justice could be made peacefully. Booker T. Washington felt the best place for African Americans was in the rural South, where they understood the customs and the land. At the Cotton States Exposition in 1895, he spoke about his vision for African Americans, saying,

> . . . when it comes to business pure and simple it is in the South that the Negro is given a man's chance in the commercial world . . . Our greatest danger is, that . . . we may overlook the fact that the masses of us are to live by the productions of our hands, and fail to keep in mind that we shall prosper in the proportion as we learn to dignify and glorify common labor and put brains and skill into the common occupations of life...

Washington's view was popular with both Southern and Northern whites. Southerners saw that Washington wanted to keep the economy working as it had in the past. They felt that Washington did not want to change the circumstances under which African Americans lived and that he wanted African Americans to slowly blend in with white culture. Northerners believed that Washington's ideas would keep African Americans in the South and train them for factory work up North at a later time.

While many whites may have favored Washington's viewpoint, there were many African American leaders who disagreed. Among them was W. E. B. DuBois, an African American who felt Washington's view was too limited. DuBois, educated in Massachusetts, was the first African American to receive a graduate degree from Harvard University. He taught and wrote at Atlanta University, where he experienced firsthand the Southern attitude toward African Americans. In his book, *The Souls of Black Folk*, DuBois criticized Washington's concept as dependent on the charity of Southern whites, and he attacked both segregation and the South's failure to allow African Americans to vote.

DuBois believed that until African Americans were guaranteed the right to vote, they could not

W.E.B. DuBois was a writer, editor, and scholar who helped start the NAACP. He opposed Marcus Garvey by calling him "the most dangerous enemy of the Negro race in America and in the world."

achieve true equality. He felt that African American business owners, for example, could not defend their rights without political and social equality. DuBois wanted African Americans to attain the rights promised by the Constitution by working within the system. He said,

> We do not believe in violence, neither in the despised violence of the raid nor the lauded violence of the soldier, nor the barbarous violence of the mob, but we do believe . . . in that incarnate spirit of the just, that hatred of the lie, that willingness to sacrifice money, reputation and life itself on the altar of right . . . We are men; we will be treated as men.

DuBois concluded that "the Negro race, like all other races, is going to be saved by its exceptional men." He called this group of exceptional people the **Talented Tenth**—those who made up the well-educated upper 10 percent of the African American population. According to DuBois, the most intelligent African Americans had a duty to become teachers, lawyers, doctors, politicians, artists, and other professionals. He stated,

> *The Talented Tenth of the Negro race . . . must be made leaders of thought and missionaries of culture among their people. No others can do this work, and Negro colleges must train men for it.*

The Changing Job Market

Between World War I and the Great Depression, economic and social pressures kept racial tensions boiling. African American migrants continued to travel North to compete for better-paying jobs, where they also found overcrowded housing in racially restricted ghettos. As servicemen returned to the labor force after the war, jobs became scarce. Many migrants were caught between limited opportunity in the South and shrinking opportunity in the North.

In 1917, racial tensions boiled over in East St. Louis, Illinois, as the city became the scene of a riot equal to the horrors of Springfield. Again, the

After the 1917 riot in East St. Louis, Illinois, members of the NAACP held a silent march in New York City. Many people were angry that President Woodrow Wilson did nothing to ensure fair treatment for African Americans.

riot was the result of a white reaction to the increasingly large African American migrant population moving into the city. Angry whites protested that available jobs should be given to whites, not to African American migrants. The mob attacked African Americans, burned homes in the racially segregated ghetto, and destroyed African American–owned businesses.

On July 28, 1917, African Americans protested the violence of the East St. Louis riots along with other vicious acts of racism in a silent protest parade on Fifth Avenue in New York City. Protesters carried banners that read, "Mother, do lynchers go to heaven?" and "Mr. President, why not make America safe for democracy?"

Outraged social leaders spoke out on behalf of African American civil liberties. Ida B. Wells-Barnett, a noted African American journalist and anti-lynching campaigner, believed that whites would stand beside African Americans to protest the lack of democracy even if African Americans became militant in their quest for civil rights. It was her belief that "America did not have a Negro problem"—the problem was with whites.

The growing migrant population had not yet tapped its potential for political or social power. Social activists like Wells-Barnett, DuBois, Locke, and Johnson spoke out against racial injustice, but changes in the laws were slow in coming. In addition, there were few African American politicians in office. Although Chicago's African American community had elected Oscar DePriest as a city alderman in 1915, most representatives of African American voting districts were white politicians. Expanded social, legal, and political power would prove to be the key that unlocked civil rights for African American migrants.

The Rise of African American Newspapers

In 1900, there were only three African American daily newspapers. These papers were published in Norfolk, Virginia; Kansas City; and Washington, D. C. However, there were more than 150 weeklies distributed nationwide.

As the African American population in major Northern cities swelled, the need to publish newspapers dedicated to African American issues

A Good Book to Read

Black and White Sat Down Together: The Reminiscences of an NAACP Founder by Mary White Ovington. New York: Feminist Press, 1995.

This book is the first-person account of Mary Ovington and vividly portrays her experiences in starting and her subsequent involvement in the NAACP.

As long as the Negro submits to lynchings, burnings and oppressions—and says nothing, he is a loyal American citizen. But when he decides that lynchings and burnings shall cease, even at the cost of some bloodshed in America, then he is a **Bolshevist** *[Russian communist who had overthrown the government].*

Thinking It Over

1. What was Booker T. Washington's idea of how African Americans should succeed in the United States?
2. **Drawing Conclusions** How do you think newspapers influenced the African American community?

increased as well. In Boston, editor and social activist William Monroe Trotter began the *Guardian*, a forum for Trotter's aggressive civil rights protests. Trotter and other editors wanted African American and white support of civil rights issues, particularly anti-lynching laws, voting rights, and an end to segregation. In addition to the *Guardian*, some of the other better known African American papers were the Chicago *Defender*, the New York *Age*, and the Pittsburgh *Courier*.

In general, these newspapers served economic, political, and social functions for migrants. They became the voice of the migrating African American society. For example, migrants seeking work found job notices, rental ads, and church locations through the papers. They also kept up on news from their home towns, and they used the newspapers as a link between their Southern past and Northern future.

Through reading newspapers, African Americans across the country learned more about acts of racial violence. As lynchings increased in number, the *Defender* splashed red headlines across its front page announcing each outrage. Robert Abbott, editor of the *Defender*, roused African Americans to fight violence with violence, urging,

When the mob comes and you must die, take at least one with you.

Newspaper editors voiced opinions on politics, demanding civil rights and an end to lynching. Yet their views were often misinterpreted as disloyalty. In October 1919, the *Courier* declared,

2 The Birth of the NAACP

A flurry of political and social activity greeted migrants as they arrived in the North. On the practical side, groups such as the National Urban League and the YMCA helped migrants settle into their new lives. However, continued inequality and injustice in both the South and North caused many migrants to join politically motivated groups like the NAACP and the Universal Negro Improvement Association (U.N.I.A.).

The Niagara Movement

Under the leadership of W.E.B. DuBois and William Monroe Trotter, a group of African Americans met in Niagara Falls, Canada in 1905. This group came to be called the Niagara Movement. Its members discussed possible solutions to the problems that African Americans faced daily.

The goals of the Niagara Movement were to demand freedom of speech for African Americans, attain voting rights for African American men, seek racial equality, and put an end to anti-African

American violence. DuBois put into words the basic aims of the Niagara Movement. He said,

We claim for ourselves every single right that belongs to a free born American. How shall we get them? By voting where we may, by persistent [determined], unceasing agitation, by hammering the truth, by sacrifice and work.

The Niagara Movement differed from earlier civil rights groups because its members demanded immediate action. Despite its ambitious goals, the Niagara Movement failed to attract wide support. In part, this was because Booker T. Washington opposed its program as too radical. Although its ideals were admirable, the Movement dissolved by 1910 to make way for a new organization, the National Association for the Advancement of Colored People (NAACP).

The Beginning of the NAACP

The Springfield Massacre, as the 1908 riot came to be known, shocked the entire nation. A white journalist named William English Walling wrote a bitter newspaper article called "Race War in the North." In the article, he pleaded for a powerful body of citizens to help African Americans in their fight for political freedom. In 1909, Oswald Villard, a leading white social reformer, invited both white and African American social leaders to attend a conference about justice for African Americans. Villard was the grandson of anti-slavery activist William Lloyd Garrison. In the invitation, Villard stated,

We call upon all believers in democracy to join in a National conference for the discussion of present evils, the voicing of protests and the renewal of the struggle for civil and political liberty.

The May 1909 conference, which was held in New York City, drew nearly 300 leaders, including W. E. B. DuBois, Ida Wells-Barnett, activist Reverend Francis Grimké, white social worker Jane Addams, and Villard, among others. From this meeting developed a permanent organization that came to be called the National Association for the Advancement of Colored People (NAACP).

Gathering Power

A **biracial** leadership announced the basic principles of the NAACP in May 1910. White social reformer Morefield Storey of Boston was the first NAACP president, and William E. Walling was chairman of the executive committee. Oddly enough, the only African American in a key leadership role with the NAACP was DuBois, the director of publicity and research. This new organization dedicated itself to gaining equal education for all students, African American and white; to ending racial injustice; to ensuring the enforcement of the 14th Amendment (abolishing slavery) and the 15th Amendment (giving African Americans voting rights); and to establishing civil rights for all Americans.

The NAACP believed that public opinion would be the main force in achieving justice for African Americans. It took out ads in major newspapers to spread the word about violence and racial discrimination. In addition, the NAACP published a magazine, the *Crisis*, to promote its ideals. With DuBois as its editor, this magazine reported on the activities of the NAACP. It waged an active campaign against lynching and mob law through editorials, feature stories, fiction, and poetry. The magazine was so successful that by 1912, it circulated 16,000 copies an issue, even though the NAACP only had 1,000 members at the time. By 1919, the circulation reached 100,000 copies.

Many of the issues initially addressed by the NAACP involved the basic reasons behind the African American migration from the South— Jim Crow laws, segregation, discrimination, and violence. The NAACP's stand on these issues appealed to migrants, many of whom had experienced violence and discrimination. They joined the NAACP with the hope of preventing further lynchings, riots, and employment discrimination.

Active Learning: The founders of the NAACP were a combination of white and African American leaders. Take notes about these leaders for use in your news article.

Battle Lines Drawn

The NAACP's first programs aimed to gain the vote for Southern African Americans, to stop lynchings and random violence against African Americans, and to improve the relationship between the police and the African American population. Creating greater job opportunities was also high on the NAACP's list of priorities. But the reality was that there were too few people to address every issue on the priority list. Work-related problems and the economic needs of migrants became a secondary issue, one addressed more effectively by the National Urban League.

To investigate acts of racial violence in the South, the NAACP established a network of undercover agents. One such agent, a blond, blue-eyed man, became a sheriff's deputy in a county in Oklahoma. That man was Walter White, who,

Every time an African American was lynched, the NAACP flew this flag outside its New York City offices. Lynching did not occur only in the South. Hanging was not the only form of lynching. Victims were also shot, burned, and beaten to death. Lynchers were seldom prosecuted.

despite his white appearance, was African American. After he was sworn in, another deputy told him that he could now kill any African American he saw and be supported by the law. For 10 years, White gathered evidence of lynchings and race riots for the NAACP.

Under the direction of Arthur Springarn, head of the NAACP's legal committee, white and African American lawyers began the battle for equality in the courtrooms of the United States. Within 15 years, the legal committee won three important decisions before the United States Supreme Court.

In 1910, the Oklahoma Constitution restricted voting rights through a "grandfather clause." Under this law, no illiterate person could register to vote. However, exceptions were made for people whose relatives were eligible to vote prior to January 1866. Since no African Americans had been eligible to vote in Oklahoma in 1866, they were effectively banned from voting. In 1915, the U. S. Supreme Court decided the case of *Guinn v. United States*. It declared Oklahoma's grandfather clause a violation of the 15th Amendment, which guaranteed the right to vote, regardless of race, color, or creed.

Louisville, Kentucky, had passed a city law limiting where people could live. The law prohibited whites from residing in African American districts and African Americans from living in white districts. In *Buchanan v. Warley*, Warley, who was an African American, claimed that he would be unable to occupy land purchased from Buchanan because it was within a white district. In 1917, the U. S. Supreme Court found Louisville's racial districting law unconstitutional.

In 1919, during an Arkansas race riot, a white man was killed and many people were injured. African Americans accused of participating in the riot were tried and found guilty. Twelve were sentenced to death, while 67 received long prison terms. African American witnesses claimed they had been whipped until they agreed to testify against those on trial.

In addition, a mob threatened violence if the accused men were set free. The trial of these 79 men lasted only 45 minutes, and the jury declared all guilty in only five minutes. NAACP lawyers claimed that the trial was illegal because a mob pressured the judge and jury to return guilty verdicts. The U. S. Supreme Court agreed and overturned the verdict in the 1923 case of *Moore v. Dempsey*.

These three cases represent only a few of the NAACP's legal victories. Despite the court's favorable rulings, however, change was not immediate. Those opposing civil rights frequently ignored the rulings, found new ways around the law, or acted slowly to bring about change. Still, the NAACP used the law as one of its most effective weapons in the fight against discrimination and inequality.

Victory for the People

The early victories of the NAACP's legal committee spurred further efforts to change racially biased laws. Although attempts to pass an anti-lynching law were not successful, the NAACP continued to address injustice.

Early in the century, civil rights issues mostly affected the Eastern states because there were few African Americans living in the West. However, because of the NAACP's effort to inform the public of injustice against African Americans, civil rights took on a national focus. The NAACP became the designated voice of African Americans, employing two major lines of reasoning—appealing to the consciences and to the political interests of Northern whites.

Perhaps the greatest victory in the fight for justice was *Brown v. Board of Education of Topeka, Kansas* in 1954. A team of NAACP lawyers, including Thurgood Marshall, who later became a Supreme Court Justice, argued that segregated schooling did not provide equal education for all students. The ruling on *Brown v. Board of Education* overturned *Plessy v. Ferguson* (1896), which upheld Southern states' rights to establish "separate but equal" public facilities. In *Brown v. Board of Education*, the Supreme Court unanimously declared segregated public schools unconstitutional.

Speaking for the Court, Chief Justice Earl Warren said,

> To separate [those children] from others of similar age and qualifications solely because of their race generates a feeling of inferiority as to their status in the community that may affect their hearts and minds in a way unlikely to ever be undone. . . . Separate educational facilities are inherently [basically] unequal.

Through *Brown v. Board of Education*, the NAACP directly attacked the foundations of segregation. Although the Supreme Court's ruling declared "separate but equal" public schools

In 1923, the U.S. Supreme Court ruled that African Americans must be allowed to serve on juries. Previously, African American defendants were tried before all-white juries.

unconstitutional, the South ignored the court's ruling. Across all grade levels, Southern states worked to prevent integrated education. In 1957, for example, a major confrontation occurred in Little Rock, Arkansas, when Arkansas Governor Orval Faubus called in the state's National Guard to prevent nine African American students from entering the city's public high school. The governor's actions forced President Dwight Eisenhower to take command of the Arkansas National Guard and send the 101st Airborne Division to Little Rock to enforce the integration of the school.

The NAACP's success in *Brown v. Board of Education* led to more aggressive demands by African Americans to abolish Jim Crow laws. Serious efforts were made to register African American voters throughout the South, to boycott public transportation and facilities that had "separate but equal" sections for African Americans, and to establish equality.

Thinking It Over

1. What were the main goals of the NAACP?
2. **Reasoning** Why do you think the ruling in *Brown v. Board of Education* was important?

Active Learning: Take notes about various aspects of the NAACP's legal efforts to use in your news article.

3 A Different Battle

African American migrants faced many obstacles in their fight for equality. While the NAACP fought for civil rights in general, two other organizations, the National Urban League and the U.N.I.A., specifically addressed issues dealing with migrants from the South.

The National Urban League

In the 1900s, a number of organizations formed to deal with migrant problems. In 1906, the Committee for Improving the Industrial Conditions among Negroes in New York formed to study ways to help migrants adjust to their new work environment and to find jobs for African American workers. At the same time, the League for the Protection of Colored Women provided similar services for African American migrant women. In 1910, another group, the Committee on Urban Conditions Among Negroes, organized with similar goals. These three groups joined forces in 1919 to form the National Urban League.

Because they were often uneducated and unskilled, migrants were not qualified for many jobs. They faced a difficult transition from rural Southern to urban Northern life. The National Urban League recognized the immediate problems of migrants and came to their aid. This organization began job-training programs for African Americans unaccustomed to factory labor. They founded community centers for the needy, assisted people who were trying to locate housing, distributed clothing, and provided leads for finding jobs. A major goal of the National Urban League was to broaden economic opportunities for African Americans by persuading business owners to offer better jobs to African Americans.

To assist migrants in "settling in," the League taught lessons in proper public behavior, good housekeeping, acceptable work habits, and the responsibilities of being good citizens. The League attempted to ease the problems of overcrowded housing by setting up programs for improved recreation facilities and better public health. During the Great Depression, the League fought evictions of families who had little or no access to legal assistance. Frequently, the most active members of the League were former migrants who had previously benefited from the League's support.

Marcus Garvey and the U.N.I.A.

Many African American migrants found a voice through the NAACP or direction through the National Urban League. Many others, disillusioned by the conditions they faced in the North, turned to Marcus Mosiah Garvey and his Universal Negro Improvement Association (U.N.I.A.) as an answer to discrimination. To them, Garvey offered a message of African American pride, independence, and self-worth.

Garvey started the U.N.I.A. in his native Jamaica in 1914. The association favored segregation of the races while promoting pride in African heritage. Garvey arrived in Harlem in 1916 and began to observe how African Americans lived in the United States. During a tour of 38 states, he saw thousands of migrants from the South living in appalling conditions. The plight of African American migrants disturbed Garvey, who believed he had a realistic solution to migrant problems. A dynamic, persuasive speaker, Garvey had the gifts to deliver his dream to the African American world. In the early 1920s, he said,

> . . . we are calling upon the four hundred million Negroes of the world to take a decided stand . . . that we shall occupy a firm position; that position shall be an emancipated race and a free nation of our own.

A man of action, Garvey quickly tried to turn his theories into reality. His first plan was to establish an African colony for African Americans.

His goal was to have his followers, called Garveyites, return to Africa, help native people throw out white colonial rulers, and build mighty African nations.

In 1919, Garvey founded the Black Star Line. The steamship company, Garvey hoped, would develop commercial ties between African people all over the world. He intended to use both the shipping company and its profits to help establish his African nation. Garvey sold shares in the Black Star Line to U.N.I.A. members.

Unfortunately, the Black Star Line failed due to a lack of shipping industry experience. Garvey's group purchased a ship that was barely seaworthy. Furthermore, there were legal problems over the ship's ownership, and on its first voyage, a longshoreman's strike in Cuba prevented delivery of the ship's cargo. The U.N.I.A. shipping line seemed doomed to failure.

Garvey also began the Negro Factories Corporation in 1919. The corporation operated African American grocery stores, a restaurant, a laundry, and a publishing house, which produced the U.N.I.A.'s newspaper *The Negro World*. Members also took advantage of U.N.I.A.-sponsored life and health insurance programs.

The U.N.I.A. promised everything that migrants hoped to gain from their move to the North. At the height of the U.N.I.A. movement, Garvey claimed 4 million members, although a more conservative estimate of 500,000 members is considered more accurate. Garvey's army of

The Chicago Urban League interviewed migrants to find them employment. In 1919, the League found jobs for more than 12,000 men and women.

Through the Universal Negro Improvement Association, Marcus Garvey promoted African American racial pride, financial independence, and unity.

supporters took to the streets, parading in Garvey-designed uniforms. Garvey's own uniform was purple with gold trim, complete with feathered hat.

Garvey took a militant approach to dealing with white society. He avoided attachments to white political leaders and refused financial support from any white sources. He claimed in a July 1919 issue of *The Negro World* that politicians from all parties

> . . . *are all white men to us and all of them join together and lynch and burn Negroes.*

This attitude outraged many African American leaders as well as the powerful white political groups.

In the early 1920s, Garvey set off on a path that led to his downfall as an African American leader. Opposed to integration of any kind, Garvey sought assistance in his efforts to achieve complete segregation from an unusual source—the Ku Klux Klan. Garvey claimed that the KKK showed "honesty of purpose towards the Negro." Other African American leaders considered this a disastrous alliance and asked the U. S. Attorney General to investigate the U.N.I.A.

In 1922, the federal government charged Garvey and three other Black Star Line officers with mail fraud for advertising and selling stock in what they knew to be a failing company. Garvey was convicted, and, upon release from prison, he was deported to Jamaica, his native country. He continued to lead the U.N.I.A. from Jamaica, but his followers in the United States lost power, and the movement faded away. Although his dream of an African homeland for African Americans never came about, Garvey left behind a legacy of newly awakened African American pride.

The Fight Continues

The Great Migration began an unstoppable wave of events that swept across the United States. Oppressive conditions in the South led to active migration to the North. In turn, that migration filled Northern cities, created a new flow of information about injustice against African Americans, and developed competition for jobs. As migrants flooded urban centers, new problems arose that required new solutions. These solutions came in the form of political and social organizations that used the power of the millions of African Americans across the country.

The NAACP fought for justice; the National Urban League worked to establish a solid economic base for migrants; and Marcus Garvey's U.N.I.A. provided a sense of pride and reverence for migrants' African heritage.

Thinking It Over

1. What was the main function of the Urban League?
2. **Analyzing** Why do you think Marcus Garvey's ideas appealed to migrants from the South?

GOING TO THE SOURCE

Principles of the NAACP

The NAACP was formally organized in February 1910, and it was incorporated in 1911. At that time, the NAACP published a list of principles upon which the organization was based. The NAACP still follows many of these same principles today. Read these principles. Then answer the questions below.

Principles of the NAACP

1. To abolish legal injustice against Negroes.
2. To stamp out race discrimination.
3. To prevent lynchings, burnings, and torturings of black people.
4. To assure every citizen of color the common rights of American citizenship.
5. To compel equal accommodations in railroad travel, irrespective of color.
6. To secure for colored children an equal opportunity to public school education through a fair apportionment [share] of public education funds.
7. To emancipate [free] in fact, as well as in name, a race of nearly 12,000,000 American-born citizens.

   The only means we can employ are education, organization, agitation, publicity—the force of an enlightened public opinion.

---

1. What is a *principle*? Use the dictionary to find the meaning.
2. What do you think the NAACP means by "legal injustice"?
3. What are the common rights of citizenship?
4. **Analyzing** What means did the NAACP plan to employ to achieve its goals?

Case Study Review

Identifying Main Ideas

1. What injustices did migrants face in their daily lives?
2. What was the Niagara Movement?
3. Why was the NAACP founded?

Working Together

The NAACP actively advertised the outrages of the lynching problem. Working together in a small group, choose one of the other issues that the NAACP believed needed change, and then create an advertisement informing the public about that issue. Present your advertisement to the class.

Active Learning

Writing a Newspaper Article Review the notes you took while reading this case study. Create an outline for a newspaper article about the founding of the NAACP. Remember, your article does not have to cover all the details of the founding, but it should focus on main ideas and supporting highlights for these ideas. Write a first draft of your article. Make sure it addresses *who, what, when, where,* and *why.* Revise your copy. Then prepare a final draft.

Lessons for Today

Today, the NAACP still fights discrimination, but it has branched out in other directions. Says NAACP director Dr. Benjamin Hooks, "We have programs to inspire students to stay in school and get them back in when they drop out. We have drug programs and a prison project." Review the principles established in 1910 by the NAACP. Do you think the NAACP has achieved its initial goals? In what areas do you think the NAACP can still make a difference? Explain your answers.

What Might You Have Done?

The year is 1905. Imagine that you have just attended a lecture at which W. E. B. DuBois explains his idea that the Talented Tenth will "save" African Americans. After the lecture, you have a chance to talk with DuBois. Do you agree with his ideas? What would you have said to DuBois?

Using Persuasive Language

The Language of Thinking

A writer employs positive and negative words as well as images and deliberately crafted phrases to persuade the reader to think as he or she does. A critical reader carefully weighs the words an author uses and analyzes the meaning and feeling behind the words chosen.

John Hope was born in Georgia in 1868 and educated in the North at Worcester Academy and Brown University. Hope openly disagreed with Booker T. Washington's views regarding success for African Americans. The following passage voices Hope's views on the pursuit of equality. Read the passage and look for words the writer used to persuade the reader.

> I regard it as cowardly and dishonest for any of our colored men to tell white people or colored people that we are not struggling for equality. If money, education, and honesty will not bring to me as much privilege, as much equality as they bring to any American citizen, then they are to me a curse, and not a blessing. . . . Let us not fool ourselves nor be fooled by others. If we cannot do what other freemen do, then we are not free. . . . I want equality. Nothing less.

> Rise, Brothers! . . . Be discontented. Be dissatisfied. . . Be as restless as the tempestuous [stormy] billows on the boundless sea. Let your discontent break mountain-high against the wall of prejudice, and swamp it to the very foundation. Then we shall not have to plead for justice nor on bended knee crave mercy; for we shall be men. Then, and not until then, will liberty in its highest sense be the boast of our Republic.

1. **Identifying Key Concepts** What is the basic idea of Hope's argument?

2. **Recognizing Details** What words does Hope use to persuade the reader to his way of thinking?

3. **Analyzing** What simile [comparison using *like* or *as*] does Hope use to describe the actions he believes African Americans should take in pursuit of equality?

4. **Evaluating** Do you agree with Hope's words? Why or why not?

For some African Americans, Harlem was an exciting place to be in the 1920s.

THE HARLEM RENAISSANCE

CRITICAL QUESTIONS

- Why did African Americans migrate to Harlem during the 1920s?
- In what positive and negative ways did Harlem change because of the Great Migration?

TERMS TO KNOW

- renaissance
- American Dream

ACTIVE LEARNING

After you read this case study, you will develop an oral presentation about a main idea that appears in Harlem Renaissance writing and art. As you read, look for artists, writers, musicians, or entertainers to include in your presentation.

During the 1920s, cities such as St. Louis, Chicago, and New York offered new opportunities for African Americans. In New York City, a section in the northern part of Manhattan, called Harlem, became a magnet for African Americans leaving the South. The Great Migration made Harlem the largest African American community in the United States.

What drew African Americans there? Many African Americans believed Harlem offered good-paying jobs. They also thought that in Harlem they would own property and escape the hard times of the South. They thought Harlem was the "Promised Land" of opportunity. Alain Locke, an author and teacher, discussed the migration in his essay "Harlem." He wrote,

> A railroad ticket and a suitcase, like a Baghdad carpet, transport the Negro peasant from the cotton-field and farm to the heart of the most complex urban civilization. . . . The Negro poet, student, artist, thinker . . . finds himself . . . *in a situation concentrating the racial side of his experience and heightening his race-consciousness.*

The Harlem of the 1920s was filled with opposites and possibilities. A Saturday night might offer a Shakespeare play by the Krigwa Players at the 135th Street YMCA or a "rent party" with food and dancing. A rent party took place at someone's apartment and an admission fee was charged. Workers' wages were low and landlords charged high rent, so the money made from a rent party helped pay the rent. While the Harlem Symphony played classical music, jazz could be heard in the clubs along Seventh Avenue. Blues could be enjoyed from the front stoops of crowded tenements.

Harlem had its share of millionaires living in mansions, such as A'leila Walker, a business executive who ran a hair-products empire. However, most people were poor. They usually worked as maids and porters in other parts of New York City. Sometimes they lived three families to an apartment with little hope of a better life.

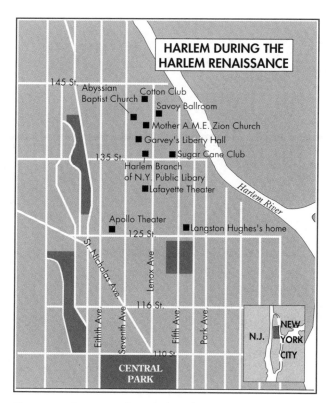

This map shows Harlem during the 1920s. At that time, it was the northern destination for thousands of African American migrants.

Sad Faced Boy by Arna Bontemps. New York: Houghton Mifflin Company, 1965. [Original publication: 1937.]

This book describes the effect of Harlem city life on young migrants from Alabama.

1 The "New Negro" Movement

Harlem of the 1920s pulsed with a new African American spirit of confidence and enthusiasm. Talented African Americans from across the United States moved to Harlem to mingle with creative men and women from the Caribbean, Europe, and Africa. Harlem offered writers, artists, and musicians a gathering place where they could develop their talents. Between 1920 and 1930, these people produced more original works than any group of African Americans had ever produced.

One New York City newspaper described the explosion of creativity in Harlem as a "**renaissance**"—a rebirth of artistic activity. The Harlem Renaissance took shape through advances in poetry, music, drama, art, dance, and fiction.

Active Learning: Write notes that explain why African Americans came to Harlem in the 1920s. Mention what they hoped to find in Harlem.

Why Harlem?

During World War I, the United States supplied England and France with war materials, such as clothing and food, many of which were made in New York City. This meant good-paying jobs were available in factories.

At the same time, the South suffered from low wages and few jobs. Boll weevils often destroyed cotton crops.

Many northern companies sent agents to the Southern states with offers of employment in the North. When these agents provided Southern African Americans railroad tickets to New York City, the number of African Americans heading North grew dramatically. In 1914, only about 50,000 African Americans lived in Harlem. Ten years later, that number had jumped to more than 150,000.

In addition to African Americans, people from the Caribbean, Europe, and Africa flocked to Harlem in large numbers. Caribbeans and Europeans had never experienced the segregation they found in the United States. They openly voiced their outrage over treatment they felt was unfair. This mix of African Americans and other cultures in Harlem fed a growing desire for civil rights.

Like many communities, Harlem had three social classes: wealthy, middle class, and poor. For the few wealthy people, Harlem provided a profitable business opportunity, entertainment, and an elegant lifestyle.

Middle class Harlem families worked hard and saved money, bought property, started churches, and became the basis of a stable African

As African American migrants moved to Harlem, city streets became very crowded. By 1924, more than 150,000 African Americans lived in Harlem, which had housing available for about a third of that number.

American economy. Many set up their own businesses, such as barbershops and beauty salons. These were often family businesses.

The poor made up about 60 percent of Harlem's population. Many rural poor who came during the Great Migration lived in run-down, badly maintained apartments. Among the lists of complaints they filed in court about their landlords were: "No improvements in 10 years," "Rats, rat holes, and roaches," and "Ceilings in two rooms have fallen." Besides crowded housing, they faced low-paying jobs, unemployment, and a life that was different from the paradise they had journeyed North to find.

Masterminding the Movement

One important concept to come from the Harlem Renaissance was the idea of the "New Negro." The New Negro Movement represented an approach to African American culture in the arts and literature, politics, and personal rights of the African American people. It was developed by leaders such as Charles S. Johnson, Alain Locke, and W.E.B. DuBois. The New Negro Movement had a widespread effect on the cultural life of all African Americans.

The Movement encouraged self-respect, racial pride, and independence among African Americans. It was promoted through several African American-run publications. One of these was *Opportunity: A Journal of Negro Life.* This magazine was started by National Urban League director Charles S. Johnson.

Another publication was *The Crisis*, edited by W.E.B. DuBois, which covered African American political issues. It was published by the National Association for the Advancement of Colored People (NAACP), an organization that fought for equal rights for African Americans.

Launching the Harlem Renaissance

Charles Johnson wrote to creative African Americans throughout the United States. He urged them to become part of the New Negro Movement. He hoped to find financial support for African American writers, musicians, and artists, and to draw attention to their work.

Winners of Opportunity's first literary awards included Zora Neale Hurston, Langston Hughes, and Claude McKay.

Johnson, DuBois, and Howard University professor Alain Locke supported the efforts of Harlem's new generation of writers. Locke praised their honesty, dignity, and racial pride. He stated his belief that literature and other creative arts could bring about understanding and acceptance between African Americans and whites.

Johnson organized a literary contest in *Opportunity* in order to draw attention to new African American writers. The editor of a national magazine, *Survey Graphic,* also agreed to print material by these unknown writers.

Young African Americans now had several places to publish their writing: *Opportunity, The Crisis,* and *Survey Graphic.* The Harlem Renaissance was officially launched.

Thinking It Over

1. Why did African Americans and people from the Caribbean migrate to Harlem in the 1920s?
2. **Analyzing** How might the poor people of Harlem have participated in the Harlem Renaissance?

Active Learning: As you read the next section, pay attention to the ideas of the "New Negro" Movement. Select one of the three major ideas (Africa, folk traditions, equality) that interests you. Take notes on material that applies to your chosen idea to prepare you for your class-room presentation.

---

2 Fertile Ground

In 1925, *Survey Graphic's* special edition, "Harlem: Mecca of the New Negro," was printed. It featured the essay "Harlem" by Alain Locke, in which Locke suggested that Harlem would provide fertile ground for an African American cultural movement.

A few months later, in May 1925, *Opportunity* announced the winners of its first literary contest. More than 300 people attended the awards dinner. The winners included Claude McKay, Countee Cullen, Zora Neale Hurston, and Langston Hughes, whose work came to represent the Harlem Renaissance.

Harlem's writers, artists, and sculptors explored several major ideas in their works. They focused on the search for African roots, on folk traditions, and on the search for equality.

"What Is Africa to Me"

One of the basic ideas of the Harlem Renaissance was the search for traditional African roots.

Among the many writers and artists who explored their African roots was poet Countee Cullen, whose poem "Heritage" best represents this idea. He wrote,

> *What is Africa to me*
> *Copper sun or scarlet sea,*
> *Jungle star or jungle track,*
> *Strong bronzed men, or regal black*
> *Women from whose loins I sprang*
> *When the birds of Eden sang?*

African rhythms drummed their way into the music, dance, and poetry of the Harlem Renaissance. After a trip to West Africa, Missouri-born poet and novelist Langston Hughes put these rhythms on paper in "Danse Africaine."

> *The low beating of the tom-toms,*
> *the slow beating of the tom-toms,*
> *Low . . . slow*
> *Slow . . . low —*
> *Stirs your blood.*
> *Dance!*

In addition, artists combined elements of African arts and crafts with African American themes to create fresh, original works. Typical of African-based artistry is the work of Romare Bearden. Raised in Pittsburgh and Harlem, he used his artistic talent to capture the meaning of African American experiences. His talents ranged from drawing cartoons to painting to making collages that focused on his own memories.

Folk Traditions

Rural folk life appeared as a main idea in Harlem Renaissance arts and literature, mostly because many writers had migrated from the Deep South. For example, Zora Neale Hurston was raised in a rural Florida town. She used her experiences in her novels to create characters and plots with realistic speech dialects, humor, and superstitions.

Here's a sample from Hurston's novel, *Their Eyes Were Watching God*. Janie, the main character, teaches a lesson she's learned in her travels:

> *Everybody must do two things for theyselves. They got tuh go tuh God, and they got to find out about livin' fur theyselves.*

Folk traditions not only influenced literature, but they also had an impact on music, painting, and sculpture. Field chants sung in the cotton fields of the South formed the basic elements of the jazz and blues performed in New York's nightclubs.

Artists like sculptor Augusta Savage and painter Aaron Douglas used stylized figures and Southern-based themes in their work.

Search for Equality

African Americans migrating to Harlem hoped to find the **American Dream**. This dream included racial equality, jobs, education, and a future. For most African Americans, this dream was not realized, and many grew frustrated and angry over the poor treatment and limited opportunities they confronted. Their anger was directed not at Harlem, but at the society that allowed inequality to exist.

Poets like Claude McKay and Langston Hughes voiced their frustration in vivid, explosive poetry. Other writers, such as W.E.B. DuBois and Arna Bontemps, expressed their rage in essays and novels.

Among the many poems that reveal racial anger is "If We Must Die" by McKay. The closing lines of this poem state McKay's feeling that dignity and courage are the tools that African Americans need to fight against segregation. He wrote,

> *. . . What though before us lies the open grave?*
> *Like men we'll face the murderous,*
> *cowardly pack,*
> *Pressed to the wall, dying, but fighting back!*

Thinking It Over

1. What were three main ideas that Harlem Renaissance writers and artists expressed in their work?
2. **Drawing Conclusions** What effect did inequality in society have on the work produced by Harlem Renaissance writers?

Active Learning: For your presentation, take notes about the work of at least two people involved in the Harlem Renaissance.

In his paintings, Aaron Douglas emphasized African American history and culture. This painting shows African American history from slavery to Reconstruction.

3 The Arts

During the Harlem Renaissance, literature and the other arts carved a lasting mark on the lives of all Americans. Appreciation for African American music, theater, dance, and entertainment grew throughout the 1920s.

On Stage

Interest in African American actors grew after World War I as plays were produced that featured African American casts. In the play *Emperor Jones*, well-known playwright Eugene O'Neill offered a serious drama with an African American in the lead role. On the lighter side of theater were musicals and revues, such as the popular *Shuffle Along*, which was the first all-African American musical on Broadway. It had been written and produced by African Americans and featured exciting jazz music and jazz dancing.

Harlem's entertainment reputation sky-rocketed when the musical *Lulu Belle* opened in February 1926. This was a powerful story of Harlem street life, which made Harlem suddenly "the place to go" on a Saturday night for African American and white New Yorkers.

Through these shows, singers and actors such as Paul Robeson, Josephine Baker, and Ethel Waters launched new careers.

Lulu Belle, a musical about Harlem street life, was a successful play that both whites and African Americans enjoyed.

All That Jazz and Blues, Too!

In addition to careers on the stage, African American singers and musicians enjoyed sudden popularity in nightclubs, on the radio, and on records. Part of this popularity was due to a new kind of music.

Jazz, growing out of the mixture of blues and ragtime that developed in New Orleans in the early 1900s, spread North with the Great Migration. The jazz of the Harlem Renaissance represented a mixture of ragtime, field chants, Deep South blues, gospel songs, and native African rhythms.

Young musicians such as New Orleans's Louis Armstrong and Washington, D.C.'s Duke Ellington came to Harlem to play hot, sweet jazz in Harlem's busy nightclubs. The CBS radio network started nationwide live broadcasts of Duke Ellington's orchestra performing at the Cotton Club. Across the United States, radio stations broadcast "Basin Street Blues" and "Mood Indigo," tunes made famous by Armstrong and Ellington.

Record companies developed "race records" that featured African American singers such as Bessie Smith and Florence Mills. This was the first time music was produced for and marketed directly to African American listeners.

A night in a Harlem nightclub offered more than just music. There was also a chance to jitterbug! Dancers would swing and sway, performing the Turkey Trot, the Shim Sham, the Big

This photo shows some of the important people of the Harlem Renaissance, including W.E.B. DuBois, an educator and writer, (in the back row) and Paul Robeson, an actor (at the right).

Apple, and the Snake Hips—a dance named after Harlem entertainer Earl "Snakehips" Tucker.

It is said that when Tucker first asked for a job at Connie's Inn, a nightclub in Harlem, he said, "Listen man, my name is Snakehips, and if I don't stop the show, you can fire me." Tucker became the first male headliner in a Harlem club who was not a tap dancer.

However, separate facilities for whites and African Americans existed in Harlem as they did in most northern cities. This was true even in the entertainment industry. For example, many nightclubs, such as the Cotton Club, limited their audiences to whites only. The top African American orchestras and high-stepping dancers could entertain in these clubs, yet they were not allowed to eat in a club's dining room or use the restrooms.

The Renaissance Ends

In 1929, the stock market crashed, and along with it went the cultural explosion of the Harlem Renaissance. Banks failed, factories closed, and millions of people lost their jobs. Because money was scarce, there were few funds for publishing ventures, and it became difficult to produce Broadway plays and stage grand nightclub shows.

The Harlem Renaissance died with the stock market crash. Yet the impact of the Harlem Renaissance on people's lives continues in the books, the music, and the art that were created then.

The Harlem Renaissance was important because it focused the attention of white society on African American artistic achievements for the first time. In addition, for the first time, African Americans in large numbers dealt with the ideas and concerns of the African American community.

Thinking It Over

1. Why did the Harlem Renaissance end?
2. **Predicting Consequences** How might the Harlem Renaissance have influenced the way white people thought about African American writers and artists?

GOING TO THE SOURCE

Views of Prejudice

Here are two poems produced during the Harlem Renaissance. Read each poem and look for the emotions shown through the writing.

"If We Must Die" by Claude McKay

> If we must die, let it not be like hogs
> Hunted and penned in an inglorious spot,
> While round us bark the mad and hungry dogs,
> Making their mock at our accursed lot.
> If we must die, O let us nobly die,
> So that our precious blood may not be shed
> In vain; then even the monsters we defy
> Shall be constrained to honor us though dead!
> O kinsmen! We must meet the common foe!
> Though far outnumbered let us show us brave,
> And for their thousand blows deal one deathblow!
> What though before us lies the open grave?
> Like men we'll face the murderous, cowardly pack,
> Pressed the wall, dying, but fighting back!

"Dream Deferred" by Langston Hughes

> What happens to a dream deferred?
>
> Does it dry up
> like a raisin in the sun?
> Or fester like a sore —
> And then run?
> Does it stink like rotten meat?
> Or crust and sugar over —
> like a syrupy sweet?
>
> Maybe it just sags
> like a heavy load.
>
> *Or does it explode*?

1. **Interpreting Poems** How are the poems alike? How are they different?
2. **Expressing Opinions** What do you feel when you read McKay's poem? Do you have the same feelings when you read Hughes's poem? How are they different?

Case Study Review

Identifying Main Ideas

1. Why did African Americans migrate to Harlem?
2. How did Harlem change as a result of this migration?
3. In what ways did African Americans change because of the Harlem Renaissance?

Working Together

Imagine that you have been hired to create a mural about the Harlem Renaissance for an art center going up on 125th Street in Harlem. In groups of three or four, design the mural, color it, and present it to the class. Be sure to include at least five ideas that represent the Harlem Renaissance.

Active Learning

Making a Presentation Review the notes you took while reading this case study. You will use those notes as part of your presentation on one of the major ideas developed by artists during the Harlem Renaissance. Choose two artists, writers, musicians, or entertainers to include in your presentation. Show a copy of a piece of artwork, or give a reading from poetry, novels, or essays that support the idea you chose.

Lessons for Today

Before the Harlem Renaissance, African American musicians had little opportunity to be heard by the public. That situation changed when musicians like Louis Armstrong and Bessie Smith made records that were broadcast on the radio. What opportunities do African Americans have in today's entertainment industry? How are these opportunities similar to those that were offered to musicians in the 1920s? How are they different?

What Might You Have Done?

It's 1925. Your African American jazz band has become an overnight hit and has been invited to perform in a famous Harlem nightclub. The club is segregated, and your band members will not be allowed to use the dressing rooms or restrooms or even to eat in the dining room. Can you think of any reasons why you should take this job? Can you think of reasons not to take it?

CRITICAL THINKING

Distinguishing Fact and Opinion

The Language of Thinking

It is important to use facts and details to support the main ideas in your writing. You should also use sound reasons and examples to support opinions. Take time to think through an opinion and be prepared to give reasons and examples to support what you think.

Frequently, writers present a combination of facts and opinions about a specific topic. You must decide what is a fact and what is an opinion. A fact can be proven. An opinion is someone's belief or judgment about something.

In writing about Harlem, both Alain Locke and James Weldon Johnson voiced many opinions. For example, Locke described Harlem as "another statue of liberty on the landward side of New York." He assumed Harlem offered social and economic opportunities and a chance for improvement for African Americans. Was this true for all African Americans?

Below is a paragraph from "The Making of Harlem" by James Weldon Johnson, which was taken from an article published in *Survey Graphic*. As you read, look for facts and opinions.

> It is true that Harlem is a Negro community, well defined and stable; anchored to its fixed homes, churches, institutions, business and amusement places; having its own working, business and professional classes. It is experiencing a constant growth of group consciousness and community feeling. . . . On the whole, I know of no place in the country where the feeling between the races is so cordial and at the same time so matter-of-fact and taken for granted. . . . To my mind, Harlem is . . . a large scale laboratory experiment in the race problem . . . 175,000 Negroes live closely together in Harlem, in the heart of New York, 75,000 more than live in any Southern city, and do so without race friction. Nor is there any unusual record of crime. I once heard a captain of the 38th Police Precinct (the Harlem precinct) say that on the whole it was the most law-abiding precinct in the city. New York guarantees its Negro citizens the fundamental rights of American citizenship and protects them in the exercise of these rights. In return the Negro loves New York and is proud of it, and contributes to its greatness. He still meets with discriminations, but possessing the basic rights, he knows that these discriminations will be abolished.

Fact or Opinion?

Copy the chart below into your notebook. Then write whether you think each statement is a fact or an opinion. Give a reason for your choice.

Statement	Is It Fact or Opinion?	Reason
1. Harlem is a Negro community.		
2. Harlem is . . . a large scale laboratory experiment in the race problem.		
3. 175,000 Negroes live closely together in Harlem, in the heart of New York, 75,000 more than live in any Southern city.		
4. [They] do so without race friction.		
5. New York guarantees its Negro citizens the fundamental rights of American citizenship and protects them in the exercise of these rights.		

Chicago's Bessie Smith was the queen of the blues. In 1927, she was the highest-paid African American singer in the world.

CHICAGO SINGS THE BLUES

CRITICAL QUESTIONS

- What aspects of Southern culture did migrants bring to the North?
- How did the Great Migration to Chicago create a cycle of population growth?

TERMS TO KNOW

- foreman
- unionization
- block busting
- vaudeville
- color barriers

ACTIVE LEARNING

After you read this case study, you will be asked to write a short story about the experiences of a young adult who migrates to Chicago. Take notes as you read the case study so you can add realistic details to your story.

For O'Dell Wills, there were many ways to get to Chicago. He could take the train, travel in a private car, even hitchhike, but Wills chose "the dog," as Southern African Americans often called the Greyhound bus.

"In those days," remembers Wills, "Blacks had to sit in the back, behind a curtain." When the trip started for Wills in Tennessee, there was plenty of room for all of the African Americans and whites to have seats.

As the bus picked up more people, the curtain was moved back again and again, until only whites had seats and African Americans were left standing. They had paid the same fare, but even bus travel for African Americans was controlled by Jim Crow laws. African Americans could not sit if a white person would be left standing.

When the bus arrived in Cairo, Illinois, all the passengers climbed off to stretch their legs. As Wills returned to the bus, the driver told him, "You don't have to sit in the back anymore. We've crossed the Mason-Dixon line. You're free to sit where you want."

"I sat in the front seat for the first time in my life," Wills recalls with pride.

For Wills, this was the first taste he had of being treated with dignity. Like other migrants, Wills couldn't wait to arrive in Chicago, the place he'd dreamed about for many years.

1 Sweet Home Chicago

Chicago was the destination for many African Americans for several reasons. For one thing, the Illinois Central Railroad and the Greyhound Bus Line both offered routes from Mississippi, Louisiana, Alabama, and Tennessee directly to Chicago.

Family and friends who had already migrated to Chicago sent letters home and made visits to the South encouraging others to join them. These visitors from Chicago dazzled friends and relations with new clothes, jewelry, and thick money rolls. Reports of jobs that paid $2 and up per day, of well-equipped schools, and of the opportunity to escape the sharecropper's cycle of poverty all

served as factors that encouraged African Americans to migrate northward. No wonder Southern African Americans considered Chicago to be a Promised Land.

A Cycle of Growth

Migration to Chicago created a constant cycle of population growth. Between 1910 and 1920, Chicago's African American population increased from 44,000 to 109,000. This rapid growth continued through the 1920s, until the Great Depression.

The increased population supported businesses, restaurants, nightclubs, and entertainment. In the South, African Americans learned of the Chicago lifestyle through letters, newspapers like the *Chicago Defender*, and weekly newsreels in Southern movie theaters.

As African Americans became more aware of the possibilities available in Chicago, the number of migrants increased. In turn, the number of services, businesses, and retail shops that were needed to support this growing population increased as well. By the mid-1920s, Chicago, like New York City, was a focal point of African American society.

Bronzeville

The center of Chicago African American life was found along Douglas and Grand Boulevards, the area known as "Bronzeville." Bronzeville was the center for African American businesses that provided jobs and services for the crowded neighborhood. Churches sprang up throughout the neighborhood. In addition, Bronzeville provided an eager audience for jazz, blues, gospel, and theater. Small businesses, such as barbershops, laundries, restaurants, and groceries thrived beside major African American institutions, such as the Regal Theater, the Savoy Ballroom, and the Hotel Grand.

But Bronzeville was also a neighborhood of opposites. On the one hand, there were mansions, fancy hotels, and nightclubs. Yet only a block away, there were overcrowded, ramshackle tenements. Massive stone churches, like Olivet Baptist Church, occupied entire city blocks, while tiny storefront churches flourished only a few steps away.

Old Settlers vs. Newcomers

A rigid class structure sprang up within the African American community. Northern African Americans did not readily accept Southern migrants and considered them rowdy and unfit neighbors.

Northern African Americans, called "Old Settlers," formed the core of an upper class, along with African American entrepreneurs and professionals. These Old Settlers tried to escape any connection with poor migrants by moving farther south along the ever-growing South Side African American community. Old Settlers felt they were being squeezed between the white community and the embarrassing, disruptive migrant class.

Within just a few years, the Old Settlers were outnumbered by the migrants. By 1920, over 135,000 of Illinois's 182,274 African American residents had come from other states. Of those residents, approximately 42,000 arrived from Mississippi, Alabama, Georgia, and Louisiana, while about 52,000 migrated from Tennessee, Kentucky, and Missouri. Although Cairo and Springfield, Illinois, had fairly large African American populations, the vast majority of the migrants went to Chicago.

Younger migrants, new to factory work and crowded city dwellings, nonetheless adapted easily to the urban lifestyle of Chicago. They crowded into nightclubs, formed their own churches, and took part in a variety of community organizations. Said George Cleveland Hall, an African American leader from Chicago, "The new arrivals have rapidly adjusted to their changed surroundings."

During the 1920s, a comfortable middle class arose in the South Side. This class consisted of retail business workers, restaurant owners, postal workers, policemen and firemen, teachers, and skilled tradesmen. Many migrants who were new to Chicago in 1915 had become well-settled, middle-class residents by 1925. Those who had come to Chicago to open their own businesses formed the heart of the middle class.

Thinking It Over

1. How did migrants change the population of Chicago?
2. **Drawing Conclusions** Why do you think Old Settlers resented newcomers?

Active Learning: Take notes on what it was like to arrive in Chicago with no money, no place to live, and no job. You might want to include a situation that involves you as the newcomer and an "Old Settler" in your short story.

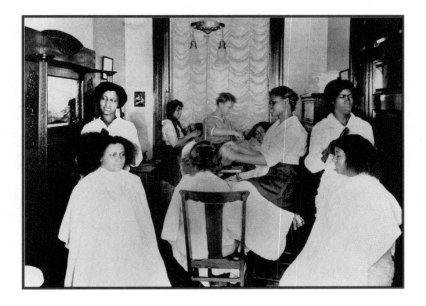

Many African American businesses, such as beauty parlors, served the needs of Chicago's growing middle-class population. As the number of newcomers increased, so did the number of new businesses.

2 New Ways, Old Ways

Although thousands of African Americans gladly left their Southern homes, they did not so willingly leave their heritage behind them. The church, a center of African American social life, was the first place to which migrants went upon arriving in Chicago. Southern-style work habits mixed well with a hunger for education, voting rights, and a better life, all of which were available in the North.

The Church in the North

As Southern African Americans flocked to the cities, large, established churches assisted migrants by finding housing and jobs, and they offered day-care services. Church members placed newspaper ads that regularly invited newcomers to join them for services.

In the early years of the Great Migration, the Bethlehem Baptist and Olivet Baptist churches overflowed with people. Said one migrant trying to attend Olivet, which claimed to be the largest Baptist church in the world,

> We couldn't get in. We'd have to stand up. I don't care how early we'd go, you wouldn't get in.

Migrants, used to small churches in which they openly expressed their religious beliefs, were disappointed with the dull services held in Old Settlers' churches.

As one migrant group said, the members needed a church "where they can sing without appearing strange, and where they can hear somebody else pray besides themselves."

Starting new Southern-style churches became important for African American migrants. Groups of migrants joined together to bring a minister from their home state. Once the minister decided to migrate, other church members usually followed. In this way, a church closed in Mississippi, then was reestablished in a Chicago storefront. With these new congregations came spirituals, gospel singing, and a social structure that linked new and old migrant families to their Southern roots.

A Taste of Freedom

In the spring, Chicago's playgrounds contained African American children of every social class. Summer found those same children on the beaches of Lake Michigan. Regardless of the time of year, ladies and gentlemen shopped "the Stroll," a strip of State Street between 26th and 39th Streets. African Americans discovered that this new-found freedom was very different from

Migrants often opened their own small churches in abandoned stores on city streets. These churches preserved the kind of worship that many newcomers were used to.

their restrictive lives in the South. But as important as recreation was to African American migrants, there were other aspects of freedom that mattered even more: the rights of full citizenship and an education.

Businesses viewed Southern migrants as customers, but to politicians, they represented votes. Unlike Mississippi or Alabama, where African Americans were barred from registering to vote, Illinois registered African American voters by the thousands. By 1919, 72 percent of eligible African Americans in Chicago were registered voters.

The full power of the African American vote became evident in 1928 when Oscar DePriest was elected to the U. S. House of Representatives. He was the first African American elected to Congress in the 20th century and the first from a Northern state. DePriest's election was made possible only by the tremendous growth in African American voting power that was fueled by the Great Migration.

Education was another draw for Southern migrants, and the Chicago school system was heavily affected by the migration into the city. During World War I, two or three of Chicago's schools were mostly African American. By the

A Good Book to Read

The History of the Blues by Francis Davis. New York: Hyperion, 1995.

This is a complete history of the blues, with biographies of the major blues singers and musicians.

early 1920s, ten elementary schools and one high school were more than half African American.

Southern schools expected African American students to leave school early or to work in the fields in both the spring and fall. In Chicago, students were expected to attend class. Chicago schools gave out bookmarks with the phrase: "Your job today is to go to school."

Not Quite Paradise

While the Chicago lifestyle was an improvement for many migrants, there were two areas that frustrated most African Americans. One was the existence of a "job ceiling," and the other was inferior housing.

African Americans in unskilled jobs had little hope of rising above their lot. Opportunities to learn "on-the-job" were limited. Since many African Americans worked on assembly lines, their exposure to other jobs within the company was limited, and a chance to be promoted to **foreman**, the person in charge, did not exist.

According to the 1920 U.S. Census, most African American men held jobs as packing house laborers, stockyard workers, porters in stores, janitors, laundry operators, servants, and waiters. Women working as laundresses or domestic servants were also held back by a job ceiling.

Because they had little education and no specific training, higher-paying jobs were closed to these workers. In addition, few unions accepted African American members during the early days of **unionization**. Unionization is the formation of a unified group of workers. Among the few unions encouraging African American membership was

As the only African American member of Congress, Oscar DePriest encountered racial barriers. Here, he points to a sign on the door of the House of Representatives dining room that means only whites could eat there.

the Industrial Workers of the World (IWW), located in Chicago.

Although African American migrants earned more money in Chicago's factories than they had in Louisiana's fields, expenses were high. Housing was overcrowded and hard to find, particularly since African Americans could only find places to live in the confined area of the South Side.

When a worker found an apartment, it was usually a kitchenette. These apartments were single- or two-room dwellings, with a small built-in kitchen along one wall. Often, five or six families would share one bathroom. The landlord would break up a house or a large, five-to-seven room apartment into a group of kitchenettes, charging as much rent per month for one kitchenette as he had previously for the entire house.

The only way to stretch beyond the restricted area of South Side was "**block busting**." Block busting meant that one or two African Americans would buy or rent in a white neighborhood. Once these few families moved into the area, many whites moved out, and housing prices in the area then became affordable for African Americans.

In the 1920s, discrimination and lack of housing limited where migrants could live. Many newcomers rented tiny one-room apartments. Still, these homes were better than what they had left behind in the South.

Thinking It Over

1. What did Southern African Americans want from the Northern churches?
2. **Reasoning** Why do you think migration rates increased between 1910 and 1930?

Active Learning: Take notes on the work opportunities your father and mother would have as migrants. Consider where they would work and what they would be doing, and include these details in your short story.

3 The Arts in Chicago

Both jazz and the blues grew out of the music performed in many places. In the late 1800s, New Orleans jazz was played by bands with clarinets and trumpets, banjos and bass fiddles. In St. Louis, jazz grew out of ragtime. One also heard the blues in Memphis clubs and Georgia cotton fields. In every case, however, jazz and blues came from the hearts of African Americans.

As African Americans migrated northward, so did their music. The blues came bit by bit from many sources: field chants, call-and-response gospel songs, work songs, and mothers' lullabies. Regardless of the source, the blues expressed sadness and struggling—people fighting the "blue devils" of hopelessness.

Blues singers with descriptive names like Ma Rainey, Jelly Roll Morton, Blind Lemon Jefferson, and Leadbelly toured Chicago clubs. Regardless of the singer or the song, the blues represented African

American emotions from Mississippi fields to Chicago stockyards.

For lonely, discouraged migrants, the blues were perfect for expressing frustrations. The blues were sung from tenement stoops on hot July nights and while working on the docks in frigid Northern winters. Blues topics ranged from bad luck to loneliness, prison life to lost love, poverty to passion.

When jazz moved North, it took on an altogether different sound. No longer the casual music of picnics, parties, and funerals, jazz became a full orchestra, with cornets, trombones, and clarinets taking the solo parts.

Whether it was hot jazz or soulful blues, there was an audience—and money—that would provide a living for musicians and singers. In turn, people flocked to Chicago to listen to music that stirred their souls and set their feet to dancing. The African American community grew large enough to support dozens of nightclubs and dance halls.

Culture for the Masses

Chicagoans looking for entertainment needed to look no farther than the pages of the *Defender*, which offered a full arts and entertainment section. Migrant African Americans were surprised to find that they could hop from one night spot to another, dance in racially mixed crowds, and attend dozens of different movie theaters. This was very different from the situation in the South, where whites and African Americans hardly ever mixed socially.

Chicago's seven African American movie theaters each showed different movies on one night. One could see all-African American productions, such as *Black Gold*, the story of oil-field workers in the all-African American city of Tatums, Oklahoma.

Live theater was also popular, featuring **vaudeville** traveling shows. Vaudeville, stage shows with comedy and music acts, toured under contract with the Theater Owners Booking Association (TOBA), which the players called Tough On Black Actors. The Monogram Theater in Chicago was a popular stop on the TOBA circuit. Some featured acts included tap-dancer Bill "Bojangles" Robinson, singer Bessie Smith, and comedian Bert Williams.

Chicago's active lifestyle also drew writers, poets, and artists to the city. Richard Wright and Gwendolyn Brooks were main figures in the Chicago literary set, while artists Archibald Motley and Richmond Barthé became part of the Chicago art world.

Thinking It Over

1. How did jazz change when it moved North?
2. **Analyzing** Why was night life in Chicago different from night life in the South?

In 1919, Joe "King" Oliver and his Creole Jazz Band brought jazz from New Orleans to Chicago. A few years later, their records with Louis Armstrong became hits.

4 Ballparks and Boxing Rings

Racial pride became the rallying cry of the 1920s, a time when African American athletes dazzled fans with their ability. During this time, William DeHart won a gold medal in the long jump at the 1924 Olympics. Baseball pitcher Leroy "Satchel" Paige struck out some of the country's finest hitters in the Negro League. In addition, in the early 1930s, Joe Louis, a young African American boxer, stepped into the ring and prepared for his role as world champion.

However, in the early 1900s, many professional sports had **color barriers**, rules preventing African Americans from participating in sports. In Chicago, boxing and baseball played a significant role in breaking these barriers; they also provided entertainment for many African American migrants.

The Negro Leagues

In the early 1900s, African American migrants in Chicago played baseball for teams sponsored by companies, such as the Swift's Premiums and the Armour Star Lambs. These interindustrial league games drew thousands of spectators.

Because of segregation, African American baseball players could not play on teams with white players, so many African American teams formed and played games all around the United States. Andrew "Rube" Foster became known as the "Father of Black Baseball."

In 1919, Foster responded to the ban on African American players by organizing the Negro National League (NNL), African American teams that played a schedule separate from the schedule played by "white" teams. The NNL was made up of eight clubs, with teams in major Northern industrial cities where the growing African American population could fill ballpark bleachers. Most teams had only 14 to 17 players, so each team member had to cover several positions. Foster's Chicago American Giants team won the NNL championship in 1914 and 1917.

At the start, the NNL was successful, recording high attendance at games and an income of $200,000

in 1923. Players received salaries of about $2,000 a year—the highest paid in African American baseball. This was an amazing amount of money compared to the average wages migrant factory workers were earning, about 50 cents an hour.

The success of the NNL encouraged the organization of other African American leagues. A Southern Negro League formed, as did the Eastern Colored League. The first real Negro World Series was played from 1924 through 1927.

Despite hardships and their inability to break the color barrier, early Negro League players looked back with satisfaction on their contribution to baseball. As Buck O'Neil, an NNL player, said,

Baseball filled me like music. I played most of my life and I loved it. Waste no tears on me. I wasn't born too early. I was right on time.

In the Boxing Ring

"In this corner," shouted the referee, "is the heavyweight champion of the world . . . Mr. Jack Johnson." Chicago's Johnson, the first African

Josh Gibson played in the Negro National League. He probably hit more home runs than any baseball player in history.

American to hold the championship title, was a talented boxer who lost only seven of his 114 professional matches. His early years in the sport, however, met with serious white opposition. White champions, such as Jim Jeffries, John L. Sullivan, and Jack Dempsey, openly refused to fight an African American opponent.

However, Australian world champion Tommy Burns agreed to fight Johnson. After Johnson won the title from Burns, Jeffries agreed to meet Johnson in the ring. The African American's victory caused boxing fans to declare the need for a "Great White Hope" to defeat Johnson. Johnson beat Jeffries convincingly. Afterward, Johnson spoke of the fight. He said,

> Hardly a blow had been struck when I knew that I was [Jeffries'] master. From the start the fight was mine. . . . The 'white hope' had failed, and as far as the championship was concerned, it was just where it was before . . . except that I had established my rightful claim to it beyond all possible dispute.

Rising Above the Obstacles

Neither sports nor the arts was an easy road to fame and fortune in the early 1900s. It was as hard to break the color barrier in sports as it was for an African American to publish a book or have a work of art displayed.

For the Negro League, problems frustrated players and team owners alike. Few teams owned their own ballparks, so scheduled games depended on working with white ballpark managers. Often, scheduled games were canceled so that white teams could use the field. Qualified umpires were difficult to find, and the NNL and the East Coast League, which were competing African American leagues, constantly stole players from each other. These African American teams traveled throughout the country, sometimes playing two games a day. On the road, Jim Crow laws in the South and *de facto* segregation in the North prevented teams from eating in certain restaurants, staying in certain hotels, and using public facilities.

In boxing, Johnson had difficulty finding bouts during his early days as a boxer. Friction developed between the white boxers and managers and African American athletes. However, Johnson's struggles opened the door for other African American fighters, including Joe Louis, who was champion 12 times. In *I Know Why the Caged Bird Sings*, writer Maya Angelou describes listening to a radio broadcast of Joe Louis fighting Primo Carnera on June 25, 1935. As Louis faltered, the crowd in her grandmother's store moaned. Angelou wrote,

> It was like our people falling. It was another lynching, yet another Black man hanging on a tree. . . . If Joe lost we were back in slavery and beyond help.

In 1935, at the age of 21, Louis had knocked out Primo Carnera. After a year of professional boxing, he was making more than $370,000 a year at a time when the average yearly salary for workers was $1,250. Two years later, at a fight held in Chicago's Comiskey Park, he won the championship.

From 1910 to 1940, professional athletes faced many of the same problems as African American migrants. Athletes faced a color barrier, while migrants dealt with job ceilings. Discrimination, Jim Crow laws, and segregation stood as obstacles to athletes and workers alike. However, once the color barrier was broken, professional sports and the arts became an avenue to success for many African Americans.

Thinking It Over

1. Why didn't African American athletes play in major league baseball?
2. **Drawing Conclusions** How do you think African American migrants' condition was similar to the situation with artists, musicians, and athletes?

Active Learning: Take notes on the types of entertainment you might have experienced as a newcomer to Chicago.

GOING TO THE SOURCE

A Bronzeville Photograph

Photographs give us a clear picture of what life was like in Chicago during the 1920s and 1930s. For African Americans moving to Chicago, housing was difficult to find and very expensive. Study the picture of a Chicago boarding house in the African American community called Bronzeville and read the caption. Then answer the questions that follow.

A young boy walks up the wooden staircase to his family's Bronzeville kitchenette.

1. What do the picture and caption tell you about life for this boy?
2. Do you think that Southern African Americans would have migrated to Chicago if they saw this picture? Explain your answer.
3. **Interpreting the Picture** What do you think the photographer wanted you to feel when looking at this picture? Explain your answer.

Case Study Review

Identifying Main Ideas

1. How did Northern churches support African American migrants?
2. How did jazz and the blues link Northern and Southern African Americans?
3. What problems stood in the way of African American athletes and performers in the 1920s?

Working Together

Form a small group. Working together, create a poster that depicts life for African Americans in Chicago between 1915 and 1930. Your poster can show pictures, poems, text from books, record labels, or headlines from newspapers. You may want to use the library for resources in addition to this book.

Active Learning

Writing a Short Story Once you have read the case study, begin writing your short story about the experience of a young adult arriving as a newcomer in Chicago. First, determine the story line or plot of your story. Next, you will need to decide if you are telling this story as a first person experience (I, we) or as a third person observer (he, she, they). Then determine what characters you need in your story. You will want to include their physical make-up and details about their personalities. Once you have these steps completed, write your first draft. Read the draft over, edit it, then complete a final draft.

Lessons for Today

There are still private golf and tennis clubs in the United States that have no African American members. The club members say they have a right to choose their own membership. Do you think this is fair? How does what happened with the National Negro League and African American boxers influence your opinion?

What Might You Have Done?

You are a radio station disc jockey in 1923. Your station has a policy of playing music by white artists only. You hear a recording of Bessie Smith singing "Down Hearted Blues," and you know this record will be a big hit. What reasons would favor playing this record on the air? What reasons would favor keeping it off the air? What choice would you make?

Understanding Cause and Effect

The Great Migration was an event that caused major changes in the city of Chicago. Some of these changes—effects—were short-term, others were long-term effects. For example, the migration brought a large African American population to Chicago's churches. Dissatisfied with Northern churches, this population founded its own churches. Developing new churches had short-term effects (social and religious opportunities) and long-term effects (a moral base in a community).

Copy the chart below into your notebook. Use it to determine the effects of migration on Chicago in a number of areas. The areas of concern are housing, education, employment, entertainment, and sports.

The Great Migration and Chicago	Short-term Effect	Long-term Effect
Religion	Migrants felt Northern churches did not meet their needs. They formed new churches, providing a link between North and South that gave migrants a social outlet.	Storefront church congregations grew and became more stable. This provided a moral base in the African American community.
Housing		
Education		
Employment		
Entertainment		
Sports		

For their journey North, many migrants packed what they could carry in suitcases and strapped them to their cars.

THE SECOND WAVE

CRITICAL QUESTIONS

■ What effect did the Great Depression have on African American migrants?

■ Why do you think recovery from the Great Depression was more difficult for African American migrants than for white workers?

TERMS TO KNOW

■ depression   ■ foreclose

■ bankrupt   ■ New Deal

■ bread lines   ■ Black Cabinet

■ soup kitchens   ■ projects

■ Hoovervilles   ■ G. I. Bill of Rights

ACTIVE LEARNING

Imagine you are a young African American who is keeping a journal. Take notes on events that occur during the Great Depression. Your journal should describe your feelings about these events. As you read this case study, look for Active Learning boxes. They will offer tips on ideas for you to use in your journal entries.

One day in 1931, Horace Cayton, a young African American educator and writer, sat in a restaurant on Chicago's South Side eating a meal. As he looked out the window, a small parade of African Americans marched by, walking three abreast. Cayton left his meal and joined the marchers. They were going to "put back" a family that had been evicted from its home for not paying rent, a common event during the Great Depression.

The first of the marchers arrived at the house and put back the family's belongings. Cayton recalls,

The woman of the house was standing . . . crying and thanking God, loudly and dramatically. . . .

Then a cry went up in the crowd. Another family was being evicted only a few blocks away. The African American crowd turned and marched in that direction. At the house, police officers stopped the people and asked them to explain what they were doing.

An old woman spoke from a soap box, talking about bread, and jobs, and places to sleep. Cayton realized

. . . that all these people had suddenly found themselves face to face with hard, cold reality. They were the people who a few years ago had migrated from the South. . . . With hard times they had felt the pinch of poverty, and now they were virtually starving to death in the paradise of a few years ago.

A Good Book to Read

Mary McLeod Bethune by Emma G. Sterne. New York: Alfred A. Knopf, 1957.

Bethune was the first African American woman to head a federal government agency. Bethune's biography covers her work as advisor to President Franklin Roosevelt, director of the NYA, founder of the National Council of Negro Women, and recipient of the Springarn Medal.

Then a squad of police officers appeared at the end of the street. Officers carrying night sticks poured out of patrol cars. The old woman yelled to the men to keep their places. Cayton described the attack vividly. He said,

. . . No one ran, no one fought or offered resistance, just stood, an immovable black mass. . . . Clubs came down in a sickening rain of blows on the head of one of the boys [who held up the old woman]. . . . One of the officers shot twice at one of the boys. . . . It was all over in a minute, and all that was left was the soap box and the struggling woman. . . .

1 The Great Depression

It was October 29, 1929, a day that was later remembered as Black Tuesday. Stock market prices suddenly plummeted, beginning the longest economic slump, or **depression**, ever to hit the United States. The stock market crash was the result of several negative economic factors. First, it had become difficult for U.S. factories to produce huge numbers of goods. Many factories were using old, nonproductive machinery that needed to be replaced in order for them to remain competitive.

There was also a crisis in agriculture—farmers were producing more food than they could sell. That meant they were not receiving high enough prices for their food, so it was difficult for them to continue farming.

In addition, many people were living on credit. When the U.S. economy was doing well, businesses allowed tens of thousands of people to buy items on credit. Banks had low interest rates, so many people borrowed money from banks. Many people spent borrowed money to buy stocks, and when the stock market fell, they were unable to pay their debts. Finally, there was too little money in the hands of the working class, which made up the majority of consumers. The combination of these factors led to falling demand for consumer goods.

In a panic, many people went to their banks to take out their savings. All over the nation, banks closed their doors because they did not have enough money to give their depositors. More than 5,000 banks closed. Thousands of businesses went **bankrupt**—financially ruined. Many people lost jobs and joined **bread lines**—lines of people waiting for free food. In 1930, roughly 4.2 million workers were unemployed. By 1933, that number had jumped to 12.6 million, or more than one-fourth of the labor force.

For African Americans, the Great Depression had actually begun almost two years earlier—in 1927. It was then that African American unemployment began to increase. There were few available jobs in the cities, and competition for those jobs was fierce.

Hard Times Up North

The Great Depression struck African Americans harder than any other group. In 1932, the unemployment rate among African Americans rose over 50 percent—almost twice the overall unemployment rate for other workers.

President Herbert Hoover called the Great Depression "a temporary halt in the prosperity of a great people." He claimed that the depressed economy would heal on its own. He refused to spend federal tax money on relief efforts, declaring

that individual states were responsible for their own residents. However, relief money given by city and state governments fell short of the amount needed to feed, house, and care for families. For example, in New York City, families received $2.39 per week for living expenses. Rent for a one-room apartment averaged about $15 per week. A wool sweater in 1930 cost $1; one apple cost 5 cents. Families could neither pay rent nor feed themselves on $2.39. In Detroit, relief amounted to 15 cents per day, and when those funds ran out, nothing at all was available.

Entire families spent their days doing whatever could be done to survive. Men peddled apples on the streets. Hungry children picked through garbage pails for food. Local churches set up **soup kitchens**—places where food was offered free to the needy. But no one was harder hit than African American migrants.

The Great Depression trapped African American migrants who had come to Northern cities. There were few jobs available anywhere, and since the South fared no better than the North during the Depression, the migrants had no place to go. Rents remained high, and eviction became commonplace. Desperate for shelter, families erected shacks from wood, old tin, and other scrap materials. Vacant lots became the sites for **Hoovervilles**,

In the darkest days of the Great Depression, New York City officials provided food for hundreds of unemployed African Americans.

communities of makeshift shanties. Named for President Hoover, these dwellings were not much different from the cardboard housing of today's homeless population.

Active Learning: Take notes on the housing and food problems of families during the Great Depression for possible inclusion in your journal entries.

Migration Slows to a Trickle

African Americans in the South who planned to migrate discovered that they had waited too long. In every month of the Great Depression, money saved for the trip slowly dwindled away, as African Americans drifted deeper into poverty.

During the Great Depression, farm owners regularly defaulted on bank loans. Banks were forced to **foreclose**, or seize, the land. In one single day in 1932, banks foreclosed on 25 percent of all the farmland in Mississippi. In addition, soil erosion and boll weevils destroyed what little hope existed for African American farmers in the South. With the fall of the stock market came the fall of cotton prices. In 1929, cotton sold for 18 cents per pound; in 1933, the price was only six cents per pound. That year, almost two-thirds of African American cotton farmers either went deeper into debt or barely broke even.

In the past, many African Americans had first gone to Southern cities before traveling North. Now, Southern cities offered no relief from poverty. There, African Americans faced angry, jobless whites who felt they should not get jobs until "every white man has a job." As in the North, many Southern factories closed, leaving more jobless men and women to go to Southern cities in search of work. By 1932, more than half the African Americans living in Southern cities were jobless.

Government Relief

Across the United States, African Americans felt Herbert Hoover had done little to end the Great Depression. In 1932, many African American voters supported the Democrats' candidate, Franklin D. Roosevelt, although the majority of African Americans remained loyal to the Republican Party.

With Roosevelt's election came the **New Deal**, the President's program to bring economic prosperity back to the United States. As part of his New Deal, Roosevelt introduced many federal programs designed to provide relief for the unemployed. While the intent of some of these programs was admirable, they actually accomplished very little for African Americans. For example, the Federal Emergency Relief Administration (FERA), the first federal agency working directly to relieve poverty, pumped money into local relief agencies. However, fund distribution was left to local administrators, mainly white city and county officials. As a result, FERA programs that might have helped African Americans never reached them because of racial discrimination.

There were two successful New Deal programs for young people that did provide opportunities for African American migrants—the Civilian Conservation Corps (CCC) and the National Youth Administration (NYA). The CCC established camps throughout the country for single young men between 18 and 25 years old. The men were paid $1 a day, but they received job training. They worked on projects such as establishing parks, fighting forest fires, building roads, clearing the land, and planting trees. The CCC put 2.5 million males to work. Although most camps were segregated, some were integrated. By 1938, 11 percent of all CCC workers were African Americans.

The Division of Negro Affairs in the NYA was directed by Mary McLeod Bethune. She held the highest position of any African American woman in the New Deal. The NYA aimed to train and find work for young people ages 16 to 24. As director, one of Bethune's goals was to ensure that funds targeted for African American vocational schools and colleges actually reached the schools where NYA students were being trained. Within a year, the NYA had programs in 25 colleges. By 1941, about 64,000 African American students were enrolled in NYA-sponsored programs and were learning various vocational skills, such as airplane mechanics.

Another New Deal program that provided jobs for African American migrants was the Works Progress Administration (WPA). The WPA had a budget of $5 billion and employed eight million workers, most of them unskilled. Between 1935 and 1943, the WPA built 850 airports, constructed or repaired 651,000 miles of roads, and erected 110,000 libraries, schools, and hospitals. WPA sewing groups made 300 million garments for the needy. The WPA became one of the nation's largest employers of African Americans, a group that made up roughly 20 percent of the workers on WPA projects.

Another positive aspect of the WPA was its support of writers, actors, and artists. A grant was given to record the oral history of African Americans between 70 and 100 years old, documenting their experiences with slavery. The WPA theater program had 16 African American units touring the country. Writers Ralph Ellison and Richard Wright, as well as artist Jacob Lawrence, were all supported by WPA grants.

Early in the New Deal, programs seemed to offer little to African Americans. Political reasons accounted for this situation; Roosevelt needed the votes of Southern congressmen and senators to pass bills funding New Deal programs.

As more programs were put in place, the federal government finally addressed the problem of discrimination against African Americans. The phrase "There shall be no discrimination on account of race, creed, or color" was added to the wording of all federal laws. Although this wording demanded equality, this goal was difficult to enforce on a local level, so discrimination persisted. However, the federal government eventually became a major employer of African Americans, with over 150,000 workers by 1941.

Most federal work programs addressed job needs for men. Jobs for women came from the private sector. African American women who migrated to the North during the Great Depression found more job opportunities than Southern African American women. However, African American women in general faced many problems in the workplace. In a 1938 bulletin for the U.S. Department of Labor, Jean Collier Brown stated,

> Though women in general have been discriminated against and exploited through limitation of their opportunities for employment, through long hours, low wages and harmful working conditions, such hardships have fallen upon Negro women with double harshness.... To their lot have fallen the more menial jobs, the lower-paid, the more hazardous — in general, the least agreeable and desirable. And one of the tragedies of the Depression was the realization that the unsteady foothold Negro women had attained in even these jobs was lost when great numbers of unemployed workers from other fields clamored for employment.

The New Deal and a "Black Cabinet"

During his early days in office, Roosevelt called together a group of African Americans to advise him. In August, 1936, Mary McLeod Bethune organized a Federal Council on Negro Affairs. The group, which had 30 members, was called the "**Black Cabinet**." It consisted of noted African American lawyers, journalists, and specialists on housing, labor, and urban issues.

This group made their voices heard on major issues that concerned the United States. Mary McLeod Bethune, who was the founder of the National Council of Negro Women, provided

Many unemployed young African Americans volunteered for the Civilian Conservation Corps. They worked to improve roads, plant forests, and create parks.

advice on African American education. Robert C. Weaver and William H. Hastie, the dean of the Howard Law School, worked with the Department of the Interior. Edgar Brown, who was president of the United Government Employees, advised on African American affairs in the CCC. Ralph Bunche, who would later win the Nobel Peace Prize for his work in the Middle East, served as well.

The goal of these advisors was to press for the economic and political equality of African Americans. They were successful in increasing the opportunities for African Americans in government-paid jobs. The number of African Americans working for the federal government increased from 50,000 in 1933 to about 200,000 in 1946. Never before could so many African Americans influence the actions of the executive branch of government.

Eleanor Roosevelt Opens Doors for African Americans

Franklin Roosevelt's wife, Eleanor, played an active role as First Lady of the United States. A close friend of Mary McLeod Bethune, Eleanor Roosevelt believed in racial equality and spoke openly against discrimination. In 1939, she brought about one of the most dramatic cultural events of her time when she made it possible for Marian Anderson, an African American singer, to perform on the steps of the Lincoln Memorial.

Anderson had planned to sing at Constitution Hall in Washington, D.C. However, the Daughters of the American Revolution (DAR), which owned the facility, refused to allow Anderson to perform. Mrs. Roosevelt immediately resigned from the DAR and arranged for Anderson's Easter Sunday performance at the Lincoln Memorial. Walter White of the NAACP reported about one girl in the audience. He wrote,

> *Her hands were particularly noticeable as she thrust them forward and upward, trying desperately . . . to touch the singer. They were hands which despite their youth had known only the dreary work of manual labor. Tears streamed down the girl's dark face. Her hat was askew, but in her eyes flamed hope bordering on ecstasy. . . . If Marian Anderson could do it, the girl's eyes seemed to say, then I can, too.*

During World War II, Mrs. Roosevelt supported African Americans' active participation in the military. For example, as an "experiment," a group of African American pilots, the 99th Pursuit Squadron, was training at Tuskegee Institute, Alabama. When Mrs. Roosevelt became aware that there were no plans to use these airmen in actual combat, she arranged a visit to Tuskegee

Mary McLeod Bethune (left) was a well-known educator. Here, she meets with First Lady Eleanor Roosevelt, who was a prominent worker for African American rights.

and flew with one of the pilots. Her trip was publicized in the news media, and the Tuskegee airmen were soon placed on active duty in Europe. The 99th came to be known as the "Black Eagles" because of the success its pilots had in escorting all-white bomber crews over Europe during the war.

Active Learning: Take notes on the NYA and the CCC for possible inclusion in your journal entries. Remember that the CCC provided jobs for single young men away from home, while the NYA addressed education for both girls and boys.

Thinking It Over

1. Why did migration slow down during the Great Depression?
2. **Drawing Conclusions** Why do you think President Roosevelt asked African Americans to advise him?

2 The Second Wave of Migration

For African Americans, like those in the rest of the United States, relief from the Great Depression came mostly from increased production due to World War II. As American men and women joined the armed services and the U.S. geared up to support the war effort, jobs opened up in Northern factories. Once again, Southern African Americans were on the move. The second wave of migration began.

A March on Washington

In the late 1930s, A. Philip Randolph, the founder of the Brotherhood of Sleeping Car Porters and Maids, became aware that U. S. factories were growing wealthy producing guns, ammunition, airplanes, and other war materials. He also noted that many of these manufacturers refused to hire African American workers. Randolph asked President Roosevelt to put an end to this discrimination, but Roosevelt refused to help. Roosevelt's actions were politically motivated; he was not willing to risk clashing with powerful industrialists to force them to hire African Americans.

In 1941, Randolph called on African Americans to join him in a civil rights crusade—a protest march on Washington, D.C. African American newspapers backed Randolph, and an estimated crowd of 100,000 was expected to march on Washington on July 1, 1941.

Fearing that such a march would cause political harm, Roosevelt gave in and issued Executive Order 8802, which barred discrimination in defense industries, government agencies, and work-training programs. The Fair Employment Practices Committee (FEPC) was put in place to enforce the order. The FEPC was created to hear complaints about job discrimination in defense industries as well as in the government. Repeatedly, the order insisted that jobs, contracts, and programs

. . . not discriminate against any worker because of race, creed, color, or national origin.

The threat of the march, which never took place, had forced President Roosevelt to guarantee African Americans the right to work. It is important to note that initially the FEPC had little effect because the law was not enforced.

African Americans in the Military

Of the more than 12 million men and women who served in the military during World War II, about one million were African Americans. African Americans were not accepted into the Marine Corps. The great majority—more than 700,000—served in segregated units of the army. Discrimination was common in the armed services, although more African Americans had an opportunity to serve their country than ever before.

Of the 1 million African American men and women in the armed services in World War II, about half served overseas. They carried out essential, often dangerous, assignments.

In September 1940, when the United States began to increase the size of its armed forces, three African American leaders visited President Roosevelt. Walter White of the NAACP, union leader A. Philip Randolph, and T. Arnold Hill of the National Urban League urged the President to end segregationist policies in the military.

In October 1940, the War Department issued a statement that said, "When officer candidate schools are established, opportunity will be given for Negroes to qualify for reserve commissions." While this did not happen right away, once the Secretary of War ordered that African Americans be given every opportunity to advance, African American officers began graduating from military training schools at the rate of almost 200 per month.

African American combat troops served under white officers. These military units contributed valuable services in fighting battles in Europe and in the Pacific Ocean. In Europe, the 450th Anti-Aircraft Artillery Battalion became the first African American unit in the invasions of Africa and Europe. The 450th was cited by General Mark Clark for "outstanding performance of duty." In Italy, 22 African American combat units—field artillery, antiaircraft artillery, tank battalions, and air combat units—took part in the invasion of

Sicily in 1943. In addition, as part of the Fifth Army, the 92nd Division pushed northward in Italy to the Arno River. Members of this division earned high honors—65 Silver Stars, 65 Bronze Medals, and 1,300 Purple Hearts.

In January 1945, the U.S. government announced an experiment—an army unit fighting in Germany would be integrated. For the first time in the war, white and African American soldiers would fight together. The unit was formed from volunteers and was highly successful in combat, with no noted racial problems. However, when the war ended, so did the War Department's experiment.

When African Americans returned to the United States following the war, racial violence broke out much as it had in 1919 after World War I. Men leaving the military flooded the job market, a situation that led to increased racial tensions. Several African Americans soldiers were attacked and lynched while still wearing their uniforms.

The NAACP urged Harry Truman, who had become President when Roosevelt died, to take action. On December 5, 1946, President Truman issued Executive Order 9808, establishing the President's Committee on Civil Rights, the first ever formed by the federal government. The purpose of the committee was to investigate unfair treatment of African Americans.

Knowing that the government needed to be a role model for integration, Truman put an end to segregation in the military in 1948 through Executive Order 9981, which stated

> It is hereby declared to be the policy of the President that there shall be equality of treatment and opportunity for all persons in the armed forces without regard to race, color, religion, or national origin.

A Good Movie to See

Tuskegee Airmen starring Laurence Fishburne and Cuba Gooding, Jr. Produced by Home Box Office (HBO) Price Entertainment, 1997.

Based on the true story of the Fighting 99th, *Tuskegee Airmen* describes the discrimination and obstacles of training for the Air Force in a segregated military.

African Americans on the Home Front

During the war, African Americans migrated once again. An estimated 330,000 migrants left the South, many moving to the West Coast where good jobs were plentiful in factories that made war supplies. Between 1940 and 1944, the percentage of African Americans working in skilled and semiskilled positions rose from 16 to 30 percent.

Wherever African Americans moved, racial discrimination followed. In 1942, James Farmer, a civil rights activist, founded the Congress of Racial Equality (CORE) to confront *de facto* segregation. CORE used methods such as sit-ins and parades as nonviolent methods of protest.

As African American migration into already overcrowded cities continued, racial pressures increased. In 1943, racial violence broke out across the United States. The worst confrontation occurred in Detroit.

African Americans had headed to Detroit with promises of high wages in the new war factories. Between 1933 and 1943, the number of African Americans had doubled to 200,000. Once in Detroit, they were excluded from almost all public housing. Most African Americans lived in houses without indoor plumbing, yet they paid twice as much for rent as whites paid. Tensions between African Americans and whites were at a raw edge.

On the night of June 20, 1943, about 200 African Americans and whites were involved in minor scuffles at Belle Isle, a Detroit River beach. By midnight, police officers had the riot under control. Then a rumor about whites throwing an African American woman and her baby off the Bell Isle Bridge caused about 500 angry African Americans to smash windows and loot stores near the resort area. Another rumor swept through a white community. According to this rumor, African Americans had killed a white woman on the Belle Isle Bridge. Fueled by the rumor, an angry mob of whites moved toward the beach, burning cars, and beating or shooting African Americans they encountered. The 2,000 city police officers and 150 state police troopers could not handle the mobs. A crowd of about 100,000 people watched the riot taking place.

Detroit mayor Edward Jeffries and Michigan governor Harry Kelly asked the President to send federal troops to restore order. The riot ended as federal troops with weapons arrived in armored cars and jeeps. The 36 hours of rioting had claimed 34 lives—25 African Americans and 9 whites.

The racial violence of 1943 spurred more than 400 communities across the country to form committees for improving race relations. African Americans were determined not to give up the progress they had made, little as it may have been.

Technology Ends Sharecropping

"I didn't believe they could make something that would beat a hand-picker [at picking cotton], but it happened," said Roosevelt Hill, a former resident of Clarksdale, Mississippi. It was 1944. The International Harvester Company was testing its

The mechanical cotton picker ended the centuries-old practice of picking cotton by hand. By 1960, mechanical cotton pickers had replaced almost all the sharecroppers who labored in the cotton fields.

newest attempt at a mechanical cotton picker at Howell Hopson's plantation in Clarksdale. International Harvester regularly tested new equipment at Hopson's farm.

A good field hand could pick 20 pounds of cotton in an hour. In an hour, the mechanical picker could pick 1,000 pounds. The new mechanical picker could pick as much cotton in one day as 50 field hands. Hopson calculated that a bale of cotton (500 pounds) cost him $39.41 to pick by hand but only $5.26 to pick by machine. The mechanical picker ended the sharecropping system. By 1950, thousands of African Americans who made their living picking cotton were out of a job. However, the International Harvester Company threw a lifeline to the South by promising jobs in its factories in Chicago.

Need for Jobs Spurs Migration

Once again, the links between the South and the industrial North were put in place. The North drew African Americans to higher paying jobs and the promise of better lifestyles. Many African Americans felt secure in the familiar surroundings of the South and hesitated to leave. However, the appearance of mechanical cotton pickers eventually made sharecropping and tenant farming obsolete. For many, migration was not a choice but an act of survival.

Between 1930 and 1950, the African American population shifted further from rural to urban living. The 1930 census revealed that about 40 percent of African Americans lived on farms in the South, whereas the 1950 census showed that the number had decreased to about 22 percent.

The shift in the white and African American populations of many major U.S. cities during the 1950s was dramatic. On the whole, 3.5 million whites moved out of cities, while 4.5 million nonwhites moved in. In Chicago, more than 2,000 African Americans arrived every week. Between 1940 and 1960, the African American population of Chicago increased almost 300 percent—from 278,000 to 813,000. The African American population in other Northern cities grew at similar rates.

However, throughout the 1950s, the North was slowly deindustrializing. The change was not easy to see, but many factories had started to use machines that could do more work at a faster pace than human workers could. Small factories began to close as larger manufacturers discovered ways to produce more products with fewer employees. The abundant Northern job market started to dwindle, and migrants to the North discovered that finding a job had become a serious problem.

Active Learning: The end of the Depression was a significant event for a poverty-stricken family. Take notes on the changes that occurred for possible inclusion in your journal entries.

Thinking It Over

1. What events spurred the second wave of migration?
2. **Reasoning** Why would African Americans join the military while it was segregated?

3 The Changing Profile of African American Migrants

The prosperity that the United States enjoyed during and after World War II did not reach the majority of African Americans. A few African American athletes, professionals, entrepreneurs, and entertainers became part of a select, wealthy upper class. A large middle class blossomed, including shopkeepers, police officers, firefighters, government employees, and tradespeople. However, the vast majority of urban African Americans still lived in poverty.

City Lifestyles

A survey of housing conditions made in 1941 showed that more than 50 percent of African Americans lived in substandard housing. For example, in Detroit, many African American homes still had outside toilets, and residents still bathed in tin tubs filled by hand. Little improvement had been made in overcrowded apartment buildings.

Still, it took years for the government to act. The Federal Housing Act of 1949, which attempted to improve housing, built "**projects**," large, multistory apartment buildings. A period of urban renewal that brought new life to the cities took place, as they destroyed ramshackle housing units and replaced them with high-rise apartment buildings. Many people at the time considered the projects a milestone because they provided adequate housing for the needy.

Education

In the 1940s, many African Americans became frustrated because they were receiving an education that did not lead to jobs. At one African American school in Pittsburgh, students hoped to find good jobs after they graduated. After graduation, fewer than half could find jobs except those involving cleaning houses and cooking meals. In Boston, a high school graduate applied for a job at a department store that listed a high school education as a requirement. When she interviewed for the job, she was informed that the position was for a shoeshine woman in the ladies' room. "Imagine," she said, "needing an education to be a bootblack."

The problem was twofold—poorly planned courses for African Americans and an unwillingness on the part of the business community to offer appropriate jobs. Courses of study for African Americans frequently fell short of the academic knowledge they needed to get ahead. Math was rarely taught in high school, while home economics often focused on teaching laundry techniques.

The Rise of the Middle Class

The step from the lower to the middle economic class was no longer an impossibility. At the end of the war, the **G. I. Bill of Rights**—a government

The rise of unionism among African Americans in the 1930s and 40s added to African American financial stability. Although some unions were still closed to African American membership, the Congress of Industrial Organizations (CIO) encouraged African American workers to join them. Thurgood Marshall, an NAACP lawyer in the late 1930s, declared that the CIO's charter of job equality for all workers was "a Bill of Rights for Negro labor." By 1940, more than 210,000 African Americans had joined the CIO. Through union membership, men and women who had little hope of rising above the assembly line were now more secure in their jobs and could possibly rise into higher-paying positions.

Financial stability translated into buying power for middle-class African Americans. The ability to purchase homes, cars, and furniture was a reflection of their economic prosperity, which brought about other changes as well. Illiteracy rates dropped; and life spans for African Americans increased.

Politics and Power

As migrants continued flocking into Northern cities, voter rolls expanded. As whites left the cities, the value of African American voters to politicians increased. More African Americans were elected to city, state, and national offices, and political pressure increased to provide equal rights for African Americans throughout the country.

The NAACP and CORE pressed for equal rights for all African Americans. In the 1950s and 1960s, CORE members participated in sit-ins, protests, and marches. They also ran freedom rides. Members tested the effectiveness of court orders barring segregation on interstate buses. Though Southern laws forbade African Americans from riding on buses with whites, African Americans rode on buses into the Deep South.

The importance of the African American vote could not be denied. In 1954, William Dawson, an African American Democrat, was elected to the House of Representatives for his seventh term, while New York's Adam Clayton Powell began his sixth term. That same year, Detroit elected Charles C. Diggs to the House.

This man protested outside a Chicago milk company in 1941. Many African Americans felt that they were fighting in World War II to preserve democracy, yet they were denied their rights in their own country.

program designed to help veterans get an education—had a major impact on African Americans. Under the G. I. Bill, veterans received a year's unemployment benefits while they looked for jobs. Veterans could also get low-interest loans for housing or to start a business. Education and a guaranteed income allowed African American veterans to move into the middle class.

Effects of the Second Wave

The second wave of migrants changed Northern cities from white communities to African American communities. The consequences of this change were far-reaching. Of the 15 million African Americans in the United States in 1950, about 52 percent lived in urban areas. Thirty years later, the African American population increased to 26 million, while the percentage that lived in cities grew to 81 percent. In 1968, only two major U.S. cities had a majority population of African Americans. That figure rose to 15 major cities by 1980.

The African American migration that began with World War II continued through the following decades, increasing the pressures to find the solutions to the problems of urban housing and unemployment. For those who became part of the upper and middle classes, lifestyles improved dramatically. For most African Americans, however, migration North continued the cycle of unemployment, frustration, and poverty.

Between World War II and 1960, nearly five million African Americans migrated from the South into Northern cities. As migrants continued to flood into the cities, an urban crisis arose. Poverty grew rapidly in inner cities, and city governments struggled to support the police, fire departments, public schools, and transportation departments needed to run a city efficiently.

On the positive side, African American financial stability grew steadily during the postwar prosperity. Small businesses owned by African Americans, like restaurants, retail stores, savings and loan associations, real estate firms, dentist's and doctor's offices, and skilled trade businesses, increased in number, adding to the African American middle class.

Nationally known companies began to produce products designed specifically for the African American market, recognizing the buying power of African Americans. In particular, the cosmetics industry offered such products as Afro-Sheen, Fashion Fair, and a Revlon line for African American women. In the publishing field, *Ebony* magazine began in 1945 as the first major African American magazine.

While the dreams of many who migrated from the South went unfulfilled, there is opportunity for the next generation to achieve those dreams. Today, one-fourth of all African American families earn between $25,000 and $49,000 per year. Just over 10 percent earn between $50,000 and $99,000. The growth of the African American middle class marks the arrival of many former migrant families to the "promised land."

Active Learning: Imagine that your family has emerged from the Great Depression and migrated to a Northern city. Take notes on urban life in postwar cities to include in your journal entries.

Thinking It Over

1. How did the population of cities change after World War II?
2. **Analyzing** What features of the migration in the 1940s and the 1950s were different from the Great Migration of 1915–1930?

GOING TO THE SOURCE

World's Highest Standard of Living Photograph

This picture of African Americans in front of a billboard was taken at a relief center in Kentucky. It highlights the struggle of African Americans in their efforts to overcome the financial problems of the Great Depression and the effects of prejudice.

1. Look at the picture carefully. Then list three details you observe from the picture.
2. What does the picture say about how the Great Depression affected African Americans?
3. How do you think this picture shows racial prejudice?
4. **Analyzing** Irony means saying one thing while meaning the opposite. Why are these words ironic: "There's no way like the American way"?

Case Study Review

Identifying Main Ideas

1. How did the Great Depression affect the migration of African Americans to the North?
2. What effects did federal programs during the Depression have on African Americans?
3. How did technology change the role of the sharecropper in farming?

Working Together

Working in small groups, create a collage about the urban life of African Americans. Decide which aspects of urban life you want to include. Next, make separate sketches of each idea. Then transfer your ideas to poster board. You can use original drawings, pictures from newspapers or magazines, or even newspaper headlines in your collage.

Active Learning

Writing Journal Entries Your family has survived the effects of the Great Depression. Reread your notes from the case study. Write three or four journal entries covering events that might have happened to your family and your feelings about these events. Review and edit your writing. Then write a final draft.

Lessons for Today

At the start of World War II, there were fewer than 5,000 African Americans in the armed forces—and no more than a dozen officers. In 1973, 79 African Americans entered West Point, 46 African Americans joined the first-year class at the Air Force Academy, and 173 African Americans attended the Naval Academy. In the 1990s, General Colin L. Powell, an African American army officer, headed the Joint Chiefs of Staff, the highest military position in the United States. How do you think the contributions of African Americans in World War II led to this remarkable change?

What Would You Have Done?

The year is 1934. You are put in charge of distributing funds and planning projects for a federally funded program. Your city is highly segregated, 70 percent white and 30 percent African American. However, unemployed African Americans outnumber unemployed whites by a ratio of three-to-one. How would you distribute the funds? Why?

Understanding Generalizations and Oversimplifications

Key Words

The following is a list of key words that may signal a generalization or an oversimplification:

all
never
always
none
no one
everyone
absolutely
without a doubt

You can use the following words to help refine or qualify a generalization or oversimplification.

almost
most
many
probably
perhaps
some
highly likely
not very likely
sometimes

You have probably heard generalizations all your life, and perhaps, you never recognized how a simple statement could be false. A generalization is a broad statement that is supposed to apply to many cases. Here are some examples: "Southern African Americans all farmed cotton." "No one cares about urban problems." "New Deal programs relieved poverty."

You have probably also heard a number of statements that are oversimplifications. An oversimplification is a statement that is only partly true. It does not give reasons or explore consequences. Here are some examples: "African Americans who don't like their jobs should just quit." "Both sides should work together to solve the problem."

As a critical thinker, you should avoid making generalizations or oversimplifying a situation. Examine the full facts of the situation. What are the reasons the situation occurred? What are the possible solutions? What are the consequences of each action considered? Is the statement really true in all cases? What are the exceptions?

Copy the chart below. Analyze the statements in the first column. Use information from Case Study 8 and your own reasoning ability to list the facts that would refine or clarify the statements. Finally, rewrite the statements to make them accurate.

Statement	Restatement
	Clarify or refine the statement
1. All African American migrants lived in poverty in the cities.	
2. African Americans had no power in Roosevelt's government.	
3. To solve the unemployment problem, just make more jobs.	

Chicago became the final destination for this family ready to embark on a new life in the North.

AN UNFINISHED JOURNEY

CRITICAL QUESTIONS

■ Why is it important to know about the Great Migration?

■ How has the Great Migration changed life in the United States?

TERMS TO KNOW

■ gerrymandered

■ Project Headstart

ACTIVE LEARNING

Many stories of the Great Migration come to us as oral history, a personal memory of someone who migrated North. After reading this follow up, you will work with a partner to conduct an interview. Your interview will explore the "story" of an African American migrant. As you read the follow up, take notes on the major changes that have occurred in the United States as a result of the migration and use these notes in your interview.

As late as the 1950s, the Great Migration continued for some African Americans. In 1953, Jacqueline Johnson's family lived on Coming Street in Charleston, South Carolina. They had two rooms in part of a house, no indoor bathroom, and a tin tub for a bath. That was the year Johnson's father Joseph migrated to the North. Joseph had received racist threats on his life and, tired of a dead-end job with no opportunities, he left to find work in the Navy Yard in Philadelphia.

For more than a year, Mrs. Johnson kept in touch with Joseph through letters. Sixteen-year-old Jacqueline, her sister Pat, and her mother finally arrived in Philadelphia in 1954. The family lived in the Philadelphia Navy Yard in housing the government had built in South Philly. To get to school each day, the Johnson girls crossed a bridge over the railroad tracks. Jacqueline believed the tracks were safer than the bridge, since the bridge had holes through it. She thought that,

they left the holes in the bridge because they knew only blacks lived in those projects and used that bridge.

Joseph Johnson had a good job as an electrician. It was a lot more expensive living in Philadelphia than in Charleston, and the family was poor but never hungry. The Johnson home became a regular haven for other family members migrating from the South. Jacqueline Johnson remembers,

My parents' home in Philadelphia became a stopover for relatives trying to get settled and find work in the North. Lives, children, and marriages were kept together and saved there. There was always movement, drama, and change.

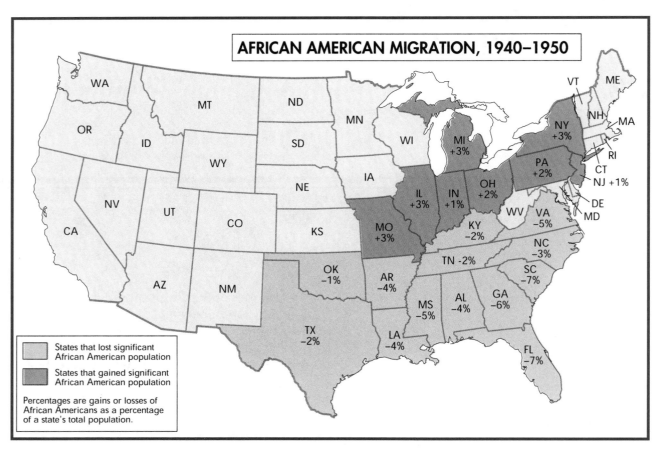

AFRICAN AMERICAN MIGRATION, 1940–1950

States that lost significant African American population

States that gained significant African American population

Percentages are gains or losses of African Americans as a percentage of a state's total population.

WA · MT · ND · MN · VT · ME · OR · ID · WY · SD · WI · MI +3% · NY +3% · NH · MA · RI · CT · NJ +1% · PA +2% · NV · UT · CO · NE · IA · IL +3% · IN +1% · OH +2% · WV · VA –5% · DE · MD · CA · AZ · NM · KS · MO +3% · KY –2% · NC –3% · OK –1% · AR –4% · TN –2% · SC –7% · TX –2% · MS –5% · AL –4% · GA –6% · LA –4% · FL –7%

Because of opportunities created by World War II, African Americans once again migrated North. Which states gained population because of the Great Migration? Which states lost population?

1 The Legacy of the Great Migration

In 1910, about 70 percent of all African Americans in the United States worked as farmers. Once migration began, the African Americans in the United States slowly shifted from rural to urban populations, and Southern to Northern locations. By 1980 the African American population had grown to 26 million people, and more than 80 percent lived in cities. This dramatic population shift has had far-reaching consequences for the United States.

Migration Brings Change to Cities

The Great Migration created a number of social situations for which neither African Americans nor whites were completely prepared. For example, the increased population in cities created strains in housing, employment, schools, health care, and police and fire departments.

From the 1940s through the 1960s, housing continued to be inadequate, overcrowded, and substandard, much as it had been in African American migrant ghettos of the 1920s and 1930s. To provide places for migrants to live, many Northern cities built public housing, homes that were intended to be used for African Americans and whites.

White residents often reacted violently when an African American resident moved into their neighborhoods. Sometimes they attacked African Americans by throwing rocks or firebombs. As an answer to this problem, many cities began to build high-rise apartment houses called projects in areas where African Americans already lived. For example, in Chicago, African Americans have always been segregated, forced to live in the South Side; so that is where the city built the Robert Taylor Homes, 28 identical buildings, each 16-stories high. These buildings became the largest public housing project in the United States. For African American migrants, the major change in their housing was that their low-rise tenements had been replaced with high-rise apartment buildings.

Migration brought change in the income of African Americans who traveled North. They made more money than they had in the South, and incomes continued to increase from the 1940s through the 1990s. However, median incomes for African American households today still lag behind incomes of white households. The average two-income African American household in the 1990s earns $33,893 per family, while a white family averages $40,433.

Since the 1970s, unemployment figures for African Americans across the country have generally remained over 10 percent, roughly twice the rate of unemployment for whites. The unemployment figures are significantly higher for African American teenagers. In 1985, when overall African American unemployment was 15.6 percent, the unemployment rate for African American males who were between the ages of 16 and 19, went over 50 percent for the first time in history.

Education, despite *Brown v. Board of Education of Topeka, Kansas* changed very slowly in both the North and the South. By the mid-1960s, only about 9 percent of African American school students in the South attended classes with white students. In the North, *de facto* segregation came into play as ghetto housing and **gerrymandered** school districts kept African American students apart from white students. A gerrymandered district is one in which the borders have been drawn unfairly to give advantage to one group over another.

Power and Progress

From the start, migrants exercised their right to vote. In 1948, Henry Lee Moon, an African American civil rights activist, spoke about the importance of the African American vote. He said,

> *The ballot, while no longer conceived of as a magic key, is recognized as the indispensable weapon in a persistent fight for full citizenship, equal economic opportunity, unrestricted enjoyment of civil rights, freedom of residence, access to equal and unsegregated educational, health and recreational facilities. In short, [voting is] a tool to be used in the ultimate demolition of the whole outmoded structure of Jim Crow.*

Voting power for African Americans translated into political power. In 1954, African Americans had three representatives in Congress.

By 1970 that number had jumped to 10, and by 1985 to 20. In 1970, only 48 cities had African American mayors; but that number grew to 286 by 1985. African American political leaders became a voice that could not be ignored.

The Great Migration affected the Civil Rights Movement in several ways. First, migration decreased the South's need for an African American labor force, which made the Civil Rights Movement less threatening to Southern white businesspeople. In addition, migration created a large African American middle class that could help raise money for the movement. Due to the Great Migration, growing black communities forced white public officials to recognize the validity of the demands of African Americans. Finally, migrant voting power elected African American politicians who became a force for change.

Contributions to the Arts

Before the Great Migration, African American culture was regional. The Great Migration concentrated talented African Americans in cities and brought creative people together. From the 1920s to the present, African American writers, actors, musicians, and artists have made significant advances. For example, no longer is it impossible for African American writers to find publishers or for actors or musicians to appear on stage. In 1940, African American writer Richard Wright wrote *Native Son*, a novel that attacked the social structure that placed African Americans beneath whites. Wright's success was followed by the appearance of such writers as Ralph Ellison, James Baldwin, Alex Haley, Toni Morrison, Alice Walker, and Maya Angelou—all of whom present the African American point of view in their writings.

Music Greats

Jazz has enjoyed great popularity since the days of Duke Ellington and Louis Armstrong. Jazz evolved into new forms—bebop in the 1940s, cool jazz in the 1960s, and fusion jazz in the 1970s. Classic blues, gospel, and rhythm and blues made way for rock 'n' roll and popular performers like Chuck

Marian Anderson's performance at Constitution Hall in Washington, D.C., was canceled when the Daughters of the American Revolution would not allow her to sing there because she was an African American. Instead, on Easter Sunday, 1939, she sang in front of the Lincoln Memorial. Her performance drew a crowd of more than 75,000 people.

Berry, Little Richard, and Fats Domino. As African Americans moved to Northern cities, more audiences of white people were exposed to their music. Urban radio stations began playing jazz, blues, and rock 'n' roll. The audience for this music crossed regional and racial boundaries.

Sports Heroes

From the mid-1930s into the 1940s, boxing was dominated by Joe Louis, an African American. Joe Louis's success in boxing was followed by a long list of other African American champions, including Sugar Ray Robinson, Floyd Patterson, and Muhammad Ali.

Sports became an arena for African American success. Baseball's Jackie Robinson crashed through the color barrier in 1946. Robinson opened the door for other baseball greats, such as Willie Mays,

Hank Aaron, and Roy Campanella. In tennis, Althea Gibson and Arthur Ashe became world-renowned champions. Basketball and football, at both the professional and college levels, featured outstanding African American players, so too did most Olympic sports.

For African American migrants who had survived the Jim Crow laws of the South, *de facto* segregation in the North, unemployment, overcrowded housing, and a lack of education, these triumphs became the foundation of legends.

Old Problems, New Solutions

The growth of the African American population in Northern cities brought about a threefold discovery. First, problems created in the cities needed to be faced and solved by both African Americans and whites. Second, city, state, or federal government agencies could not bring about change by themselves. Third, a unified effort by both African Americans and whites produced workable, livable solutions for all. Efforts to improve community life have included programs by social organizations such as the National Urban League, as well as government programs such as **Project Headstart**—an education program designed to help children get a good start on their education.

Active Learning: Take notes on the changes that have occurred for African American migrants in Northern cities. Be sure to include both positive and negative changes, so your interview will be balanced and not one-sided.

Thinking It Over

1. Name three advances for African Americans since the Great Depression.
2. **Drawing Conclusions** How do you think the Great Migration affected the Civil Rights Movement?

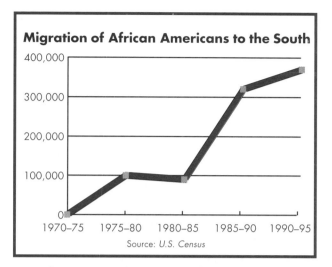

Migration of African Americans to the South

Source: U.S. Census

From the 1980s to the present, African Americans have been migrating South.

2 Going "Back Home"

Today, many African Americans are reversing the trend of the Great Migration and moving from the North to the South. They are headed South for the same reasons as whites—warmer weather, cheaper housing, growing job markets, and what they believe is a better way of life. The dream for African Americans has not changed, but the place to achieve the dream has switched from North to South.

Going Back Home

A surprising trend began late in the 1980s—a reverse migration to the South. As industrial centers moved factories southward to escape high taxes, high utility expenses, and union labor costs, job opportunities in the North dwindled. African Americans and whites found better job opportunities in Southern cities.

U.S. Census Bureau reports show that between 1990 and 1996, the South saw gains of African American migrants from the Northeast, Midwest, and West. During the first half of the 1990s, the South gained 368,000 African American migrants. At the same time, the Northeast lost

233,600 African Americans while about 107,000 left the Midwest and about 30,000 left the West.

African Americans are finding that the cost of housing and taxes is less in the South than in the North. The problems of segregation and discrimination of the old South are no longer major issues—or, at the very least, they are not much different from the problems in the North. For many African Americans, the "one-way" ticket North has been exchanged for a "one-way" ticket back home.

Lasting Legacy

The Great Migration's legacy for the United States is varied and changeable. African American migrants continue to be "on the move," bringing cultural and racial diversity to every region of the United States. As African American political leader Malcolm X once said,

> We are not fighting for integration, nor are we fighting for separation. We are fighting for recognition as human beings. We are fighting for . . . human rights.

A new job focus for individuals and organizations that fought for civil rights and a recognition of the rights of African Americans are all part of the legacy of the Great Migration.

Active Learning: Take notes on the reverse migration to the South for use in your interview. Consider what positives and negatives influence a decision to migrate today.

In Chicago, a statue honors the millions of African Americans who journeyed North during the Great Migration. The metal statue is made up of little sections that look like the soles of shoes.

Thinking It Over

1. What reasons are given for reverse migration?
2. **Analysis** Why might African Americans be more successful in the South today than they would have been in the 1950s?

Follow-Up Review

Identifying Main Ideas

1. How has the Great Migration continued to affect cities?
2. What are some of the African American contributions to popular culture?
3. How did the Great Migration affect civil rights?

Working Together

Very few people live their entire lives in the same city or town. In some ways, we are all migrants from one area to another. Working in small groups, discuss your family's history, places you or others in your family may have lived, and experiences you may have encountered when migrating from one place to another. Make a map showing the migration patterns of each family in your group, using a different color to designate each family's movements.

Active Learning

Conducting an Interview Work in pairs, with one person doing the interview and the other role-playing an African American migrant. Based on material in this case study, write a list of ten questions covering both positive and negative aspects of being a migrant. Use questions that answer "what," "why," or "how," so that responses are not limited to "yes" and "no" answers. Role-play your interview in front of the class.

Lessons for Today

In his inaugural address as governor of Georgia, former President Jimmy Carter said, "No poor, rural, weak or black person should ever again have to bear the additional burden of being deprived of the opportunity for an education, a job or simple justice." How do you think African Americans moving to the South feel about their opportunities there? Explain your answer.

What Would You Have Done?

The year is 1955. Imagine you are an African American doctor working at a large urban hospital in Detroit. You are offered a promotion to chief-of-staff in a hospital in a mid-sized, all-white Michigan city about 4 hours away. What reasons would favor taking the job? What reasons would be against it? What choice would you make?

GLOSSARY

American Dream an outlook for the United States that includes racial equality, jobs, education, and a future (p. 82)

bankrupt financially ruined (p. 103)

biracial two races (p. 68)

Black Cabinet a group of African American advisors to President Franklin Delano Roosevelt (p. 105)

block busting one or two African Americans buying or renting in a white neighborhood (p. 94)

boll weevil an insect that lays its eggs in cotton bolls; the larva destroy the cotton from the inside (p. 14)

Bolshevist a member of the Russian communist group that overthrew the government (p. 67)

boycotts refusals to buy, sell, or use something until particular demands are met (p. 43)

bread lines lines of people waiting for free foods (p. 103)

chain migration the process by which communities are joined together again as families and friends move to a new location (p. 38)

circulation the number of newspapers or magazines sold within a given period (p. 31)

color barriers rules preventing African Americans from participating in sports (p. 96)

cost of living the average price of housing, food, clothes, medical care, and other essentials in a specific area (p. 9)

de facto segregation the unwritten practice of keeping African Americans and whites separate (p. 43)

depression an economic slump (p. 102)

destination the place to which a person goes (p. 40)

discrimination treating one group of people better than another group (p. 53)

domestic servants people who work in private homes, like maids or cleaning women (p. 53)

Emancipation Proclamation a federal document that abolished slavery in the South (p. 6)

entrepreneurs people who start and manage their own businesses (p. 55)

exodus the Biblical word for departure (p. 31)

Exodusters African Americans migrating to the West, named after the Book of Exodus (p. 21)

foreclose to seize land from owners who cannot pay their bills (p. 104)

foreman the person in charge in a factory department or work group (p. 93)

franchise the right to vote (p. 15)

gerrymandered a district in which the borders have been drawn unfairly to give advantage to one group over another (p. 119)

G. I. Bill of Rights a federally funded program for education, housing, and job training for servicemen who left the military after the war (p. 111)

ghettos areas in which a group of people reside, usually forced to do so by others (p. 43)

Great Migration a shift in the African American population from the rural South to the urban North (p. 6)

Hoovervilles groups of ramshackle, make-shift shacks during the Depression (p. 103)

immigrants people who move into another country to live (p. 26)

industrialists manufacturers (p. 27)

industrialized an economy that is based on manufacturing (p. 20)

interest money a person has to pay on a loan or debt (p. 13)

lynching a mob illegally seizing and killing a suspected criminal or troublemaker (p. 18)

migrants people who move from one place to another (p. 38)

migration moving from one country or region to another (p. 5)

New Deal President Franklin Delano Roosevelt's plan to ease economic suffering (p. 104)

productivity the amount of output per worker (p. 51)

Project Headstart an education program designed to help children get a good start on their education (p. 121)

projects public housing buildings (p. 111)

propaganda false or distorted information (p. 19)

Reconstruction rebuilding the South after the Civil War (p. 6)

recruiters people whose job it is to get others to join something or to do something in particular (p. 27)

renaissance a rebirth of learning, arts, and culture (p. 79)

segregated kept races separate from each other (p. 15)

sharecropper farmer who worked the land to receive a share of the money made after the sale of the harvested crop (p. 26)

sharecropping a system in which farmers worked the land to receive a share of the money after the sale of a harvested crop (p. 12)

soup kitchens places where food is offered free to the needy (p. 103)

strikebreakers workers hired specifically to stop a strike (p. 55)

Talented Tenth the well-educated upper 10 percent of the African American population (p. 65)

Thirteenth Amendment the Amendment to the Constitution that abolished slavery (p. 6)

unionization the formation of a unified group of workers (p. 93)

vaudeville live entertainment with music, dancing, and comedy sketches (p. 95)

ACKNOWLEDGMENTS

Grateful acknowledgment is made to the following publishers, authors, and other copyright holders:

p. 24: From COLORED PEOPLE by Henry Louis Gates Jr. Copyright © 1994 by Henry Louis Gates Jr. Reprinted by permission of Alfred A. Knopf Inc.

p. 46: EXCERPT from AMERICAN HUNGER by RICHARD WRIGHT. Copyright © 1944 by Richard Wright. Copyright © 1977 by Ellen Wright. Reprinted by permission of HarperCollins Publishers, Inc.

p. 85: Globe Fearon Educational Publisher has executed a reasonable and concerted effort to contact the copyright holder of the poem "If We Must Die" from THE COLLECTED POEMS OF CLAUDE McKAY. Globe Fearon Educational Publisher eagerly invites any persons knowledgeable about the whereabouts of the authors or agents to contact Globe Fearon Educational Publisher to arrange for the customary publishing transactions.

p. 85: From COLLECTED POEMS by Langston Hughes. Copyright © 1994 by the Estate of Langston Hughes. Reprinted by permission of Alfred A. Knopf Inc.

Grateful acknowledgment is made to the following for illustrations, photographs, and reproductions on the pages indicated:

Photo credits: **Cover:** Library of Congress; **Cover (Inset):** Amistad Research Center; **p. 5:** Library of Congress; **p. 7:** Library of Congress; **p. 9:** Library of Congress; **p. 10:** Library of Congress; **p. 11:** Library of Congress; **p. 13:** Corbis-Bettmann; **p. 15:** Corbis-Bettmann; **p. 17:** Florida State Archives; **p. 18:** The Granger Collection; **p. 19:** Rutherford B. Hayes Presidential Center; **p. 20:** The Granger Collection; **p. 21:** Kansas State Historical Society; **p. 25:** Library of Congress; **p. 27:** Corbis-Bettmann; **p. 28:** Library of Congress; **p. 29:** Library of Congress; **p. 30:** Library of Congress; **p. 32:** Culver Pictures; **p. 33:** The Chicago Defender; **p. 37:** The Florida State Archives; **p. 39:** Archive Photos; **p. 44:** University of Illinois at Chicago, The University Library, Department of Special Collections, Arthur Aldis Papers; **p. 45:** Chicago Historical Society; **p. 49:** Mississippi Department of Archives and History; **p. 50:** Reproduced from the collections of the Ohio Historical Society; **p. 51:** UPI/Corbis-Bettmann; **p. 52:** National Archives; **p. 53:** The Western Reserve Historical Society; **p. 55:** Brown Brothers; **p. 56:** Corbis-Bettmann; **p. 58:** The Western Reserve Historical Society; **p. 63:** UPI/Corbis-Bettmann; **p. 65:** UPI/Corbis-Bettmann; **p. 66:** Corbis-Bettmann; **p. 69:** University of Illinois at Chicago, The University Library, Chicago Urban League Records; **p. 70:** UPI/Corbis-Bettmann; **p. 72:** UPI/Corbis-Bettmann; **p. 73:** UPI/Corbis-Bettmann; **p. 77:** Schomburg Center for Research in Black Culture; **p. 79:** Schomburg Center for Research in Black Culture; **p. 80:** Williamson Collection, Moorland Springarn Research Center; **p. 82:** Aaron Douglas; **p. 83:** Billy Rose Theater Collection, New York Public Library at Lincoln Center, Astor, Lenox, and Tilden Foundations; **p. 84:** Schomburg Center for Research in Black Culture; **p. 89:** Archive Photos/Frank Driggs Collection; **p. 91:** Corbis-Bettmann; **p. 92:** Library of Congress; **p. 93:** Corbis-Bettmann; **p. 94:** Schomburg Center for Research in Black Culture; **p. 95:** Schomburg Center for Research in Black Culture; **p. 96:** Library of Congress; **p. 98:** Schomburg Center for Research in Black Culture; **p. 101:** Library of Congress; **p. 103:** Corbis-Bettmann; **p. 105:** Bettmann Archive; **p. 106:** Corbis-Bettmann; **p. 107:** Corbis-Bettmann; **p. 108:** Brown Brothers; **p. 112:** Library of Congress; **p. 114:** Margaret Bourke-White, Life Magazine © Time Inc.; **p. 117:** Stock Montage/Historical Pictures Collection; **p. 120:** UPI/Corbis-Bettmann; **p. 122:** Paul Merideth